Clifford Olson

The Beast of British Columbia

CRIMES CANADA:

True Crimes That Shocked The Nation

~ Volume 12 ~

by Elizabeth Broderick

Clifford Olson

The Beast of British Columbia

CRIMES CANADA:

True Crimes That Shocked The Nation

~ Volume 12 ~

by Elizabeth Broderick

www.CrimesCanada.com

ISBN-13: 978-1523718474
ISBN-10: 1523718471

Copyright and Published (02.2016)

VP Publications an imprint of

RJ Parker Publishing, Inc.

Published in Canada

Copyrights

Kindle Unlimited

Enjoy these top-rated true crime eBooks from VP Publications **FREE** as part of your Kindle Unlimited subscription. You can read it on your Kindle Fire, on a computer via Kindle Cloud Reader or on any smartphone with the free Kindle reading app.

OR

Click 'Buy' and own your copy.

View All Books by RJ Parker Publishing at the following Amazon Links:

Amazon Kindle - USA

Amazon Kindle - Canada

Amazon Kindle - UK

Amazon Kindle - Australia

View Crimes Canada Book at:

rjpp.ca/CC-CRIMES-CANADA-BOOKS

Table of Contents

A Close Call For The Rat

February 13, 1976: A crowd had gathered around a poker game in the game room of Saskatchewan's Prince Albert Penitentiary. One of the players was 36-year-old Clifford Robert Olson. Olson had just recently transferred to this prison from another penitentiary in British Columbia. Prince Albert was supposed to provide better protection for inmates considered to be targets for violence. Olson's reputation certainly made him a target. Amongst the culture of these inmates, he was known to be a child molester (otherwise called a "skinner"), as well as a rat (informer). While criminals are not often thought to be the most morally rigid people, they do have their own set of moral codes to follow. These include keeping out of other people's business, not cooperating with the authorities, and knowing your place in the hierarchy. Olson was not like most inmates, however. The only rule he followed was to serve his own impulses, even when they meant trouble later. Considering the new level of protection he was supposed to receive, he was happy to be transferred while continuing to apply for parole.

Still, on this particular night Olson felt uneasy. He had only been in the prison for 10 days and while he had been there twice before, he felt less comfortable this time. A man from the neighboring cell, Windsor Chalifoux, invited Olson to join him and four others for the game. As the game progressed, Olson couldn't help but notice other men who had come into the room to watch. One group of guys was particularly bothering him. He only knew one of the men, a guy named Harvey who was in for murder. Harvey was joined by George Lancaster, Pat Noonan, and Gordon Lussier. The atmosphere in the room became quite tense as Olson's paranoia escalated. Finally, one of the men asked to join in the game.

Olson responded by saying, "Go start your own game." The man took the opportunity to call Olson out for being a rat back in the B.C. Penitentiary. Olson had garnered himself a reputation for helping prison authorities find out which inmates had drugs. Such behavior made him unpopular amongst his prison mates. Olson angrily denied being a rat. Seeing that no one at the table would back him up, he decided to cash in his chips and began to walk away.

Suddenly he noticed George Lancaster had run in front of him down the corridor. Olson was trapped. He went for Gordon Lussier and they attacked each other. Olson managed to catch Lussier's punch and knock him down with his own. However, Lussier had been holding a pair of scissors, which still found their way into Olson's left arm.

Olson ran away from Lussier, but was caught by the rest of the group. They held him while Pat Noonan stabbed him with a knife. Despite being outnumbered, Olson managed to break free only to be stabbed again in the back by Lussier's scissors. The gang beat and kicked Olson, with the full intention of murdering him.

Unfortunately for his future victims, Olson managed to escape this attempt on his life. Years later in 2011, Gordon Lussier would be interviewed by Sun News about the incident. The reporter looked on sympathetically as Lussier described being approached by other inmates to kill Olson. Supposedly, they wanted to kill him for forcing a young prisoner into being a sex slave. It is likely that Lussier used this different storyline to make himself redeemable in the eyes of viewers. However, it did not matter which story he used. Even a murderer like Lussier would look virtuous compared to Clifford Olson. Lussier told Sun News that he regretted not being able to successfully kill Olson - a sentiment shared by most Canadians.

A Rather Normal Childhood

Clifford Olson was born in Vancouver on the first day of 1940. His parents were Clifford Olson Sr. and Leona Gariepy. His father was a soldier for the Canadian Army and his mother was a meatpacker. The couple was unmarried at the time, and therefore baby Olson was considered a bastard.

For the first three years of his life, Olson lived with his mother while his father was at war. The duo moved from Vancouver to Vancouver Island and then onto Edmonton to be near Leona's family. With no father and an overly indulgent mother, Olson was a disobedient child from the start. He would manipulate and lie to any adults who tried to discipline him. He had attractive looks, which he used to his advantage for as long as they lasted.

Clifford Sr. returned to Canada in 1945. The family then moved back to British Columbia to live in Richmond. They later had three more children: Sharon, Richard, and Dennis. Aside from his sister, whom he molested, Olson did not have much of a relationship with his siblings. He also didn't have a particularly great relationship with his father. Clifford Sr. had openly shown a stronger bond with the other three children. Perhaps it was because Olson was so close with his mother.

Olson would later reflect on his childhood as being rather normal, although he also claimed to experience sexual abuse at the hands of an uncle. The uncle was supposedly a teenager at the time of the abuse. He would molest and rape both Olson and his cousin, Marlene. Afterwards the uncle would give both children money so that they wouldn't tell anyone what had happened.

Olson's wife, Joan, later said that she believed that Olson had actually been sexually abused by his father. She was suspicious initially because Olson had never identified who this uncle was to her. In his typically flippant manner, Olson said that his experiences were "nothing" and that "I was bum fucked, but there was no penetration". While Olson did admit he received corporal punishment from his father, he angrily denied Joan's accusation that his father's abuse was also sexual in nature. Whenever Joan tried to broach that possibility with him, he angrily denied it. Nonetheless, his own experiences of sexual abuse would give some reasoning as to why Olson became a pedophile. Many psychologists note the link that most pedophiles are sexually abused as children themselves.

Pedophilic behavior is most likely to begin in the teenage years of the perpetrator. For Olson, his sexual aggressiveness was already developed by the time he was ten years old. He would use a knife to threaten girls into letting him molest them. He even forced this upon his own younger sister, Sharon. Despite this, Sharon would later aid Clifford in imprisoning a girlfriend that he traumatically abused. Like most of the women who knew him, she was also unable to resist his manipulative personality.

Aside from being a sexual predator, Olson was also an excellent thief and swindler. This was another behavior that began at a young age. Some of his earliest and fondest memories are of pulling off scams. One of these scams was inspired by a day of joining his father on his job as a milkman. Noticing that people would leave money for the milk outside their houses, Olson resolved to get up before his father left at dawn in order to steal the money first. He found success with this tactic and decided to try his luck at stealing from other milkmen. He would discreetly follow them on their routes. When a milkman would walk up to a house to deliver milk, Olson would sneak into their cart and steal the money they had collected.

Olson remained a con artist throughout his whole life. His preferred scam as an adult entailed buying items from stores and getting a refund by grabbing the identical item from off of the shelves. This way, he would get to keep the item while also getting a full refund for it. He would usually then resell the items elsewhere at a discounted price. It was through these means that Olson would always have money. He was noted for being generous with his money because he always knew he could get more. Whenever he was not in prison, Olson made scamming his full time job. He would devise elaborate, clever schemes that he would repeat over and over again. Often the effort put into scamming was as much as if he was earning the money through work.

Olson never felt real remorse for scamming any more than he did for the murders for which he was later charged. Whenever he was caught misbehaving as a child, Olson's mother would try to keep his bad behavior a secret from his father. She was worried that any kind of discipline to her favorite child would become abusive. One can sympathize with a mother trying to protect her child from violence. However, the result of his mother's fawning was that Olson learned at a young age how to manipulate himself out of trouble, and especially with women.

Joan even believed that Olson's mother knew about the murder of 16-year-old Daryn Johnsrude before the police caught Olson. The night of Daryn's murder, Olson told his parents something that made them cry. Whenever Joan tried to ask his mother what he had said, she would begin crying and refuse to answer. It was only much later that Joan realized the date coincided with the night of Daryn's murder.

In his early teen years, Olson got his first legitimate job at a horse racing track.

He had skipped school so much to hang around at the track and gamble, it seemed natural for him to work there. The environment of gambling and excitement was a perfect fit for him. Olson's job consisted of taking the horses for walks after races to help them slowly come down from the intensity of the race. His real interest in the job was the opportunity to steal wallets from other employees. Nonetheless, this job was one of the few relatively normal things he did to participate in society.

Prison, Rape, and Other Antisocial Behavior

In 1957, Olson had his first of many turns in prison. While breaking into a woodworking factory in Richmond, he was seen by a couple and reported to the RCMP (Royal Canadian Mounted Police). After a brief chase, Olson was caught and later sent to the New Haven Borstal Institution. The Institution was based on a system of rehabilitation as opposed to the typical punitive environment of the correctional system. At the New Haven Institution, young offenders were separated from older criminals. The idea was that this system would shield some of the younger offenders from the realities of criminal life in hopes that they might choose another path.

In Olson's case, he opted to break out of the institution. Along with two friends, he managed to get to the Fraser River and steal a boat. They headed for Vancouver, but eventually they required rescuing by another boat on the river. However, by that time the RCMP was onto them. Olson still managed to evade them long enough to return to his parents' house. His parents convinced him to turn himself in at the closest police station, and surprisingly he took that advice. Olson was given a one-year sentence at Oakalla prison, with his parole due for April 1959.

In 1959, Olson began his first homosexual relationship. One day he came upon an underage inmate being sexually abused by two older inmates. Rather than helping this boy, Olson joined in the acts of abuse. Strangely, Olson and Lorne Johnson somehow became romantic partners.

Studies have shown that one of the biggest predictors for sexual abuse in romantic relationships is a history of familial abuse for either person in the relationship. It is unknown if this was true for Johnson, but it certainly was for Olson. His experience of familial abuse made him prone to perpetrating violence on others who felt close to him.

What is particularly unusual about their relationship was that it started on a level of extreme abuse and then developed into something more romantic. Typically, abusive relationships begin on a healthier, romantic note. As comfort and attachment increase, abuse begins. Regardless of Johnson's reasons for staying, the two certainly portrayed themselves to be seriously involved in each other. They managed to sneak a secret wedding while imprisoned, and exchanged their own rings handmade from copper pipes. Upon release, Johnson stayed with Olson's family. Their romantic relationship remained a secret during that time.

Some question the validity of these types of romantic relationships for Olson. His psychological and behavioral traits show that he consistently related to other people in an entirely exploitative manner. Olson is a perfect fit for the conditions of Antisocial Personality Disorder. The American Psychiatric Association is responsible for putting out frequently updated manuals that describe the characteristics and criteria for various psychiatric disorders.

As of 2013, the diagnostic criteria for Antisocial Personality Disorder include:

A pervasive pattern of disregard for and violation of the rights of others, occurring since age 15 years, as indicated by three or more of the following:

1. Failure to conform to social norms with respect to lawful behaviors, as indicated by repeatedly performing acts that are grounds for arrest.

2. Deceitfulness, as indicated by repeated lying, use of aliases, or conning others for personal profit or pleasure.

3. Impulsivity or failure to plan ahead.

4. Irritability and aggressiveness, as indicated by repeated physical fights or assaults.

5. Reckless disregard for the safety of others.

6. Consistent irresponsibility, as indicated by repeated failure to sustain consistent work behavior or honor financial obligations.

7. Lack of remorse, as indicated by being indifferent to or rationalizing having hurt, mistreated, or stolen from another.

The DSM 5 (*Diagnostic and Statistical Manual of Mental Disorders,*

Fifth Edition) then goes on to describe the behavioral patterns of Antisocial Personality Disorder as being considered analogous to the terms psychopathy, sociopathy, or dissocial personality disorder.

Throughout his life, Olson's romantic and sexual relationships were characterized by these traits of manipulation, aggression, and disinhibition. He would manipulate both males and females into remaining in abusive relationships with him. Even when he was married, Olson would risk bringing home teenagers to have sex with him in the house. He knew that Joan would be upset by this behavior. However, he also knew that she was completely under his control.

Joan had threatened to leave Olson several times throughout their relationship. As her dependency on him grew, she found she could not follow through on her desire to leave. Olson was the father of Joan's child and she relied on him financially. As time went on, Joan began to intentionally ignore that Olson was likely having affairs. However, it was another thing for Joan to ignore an affair when it was happening in her own home.

One particular example was a young man named Randy Ludlow. Randy was 18 and homeless when he first met Olson. After fighting with his stepdad, Randy was kicked out of his home. He decided to seek out his biological father, whom he had never met.

Randy was hitchhiking on the King George Highway when Olson stopped the car. After only a few minutes, Randy discovered that Olson had been friends with his father when they were both younger. Olson offered to help Randy locate his father. It seemed very serendipitous.

Olson let Randy stay in their house despite Joan's protestations. He used Randy as an accomplice for stealing as well as a sexual partner. Joan felt that Randy was envious of her because he would be rude and threatening towards her in private.

Eventually Joan's suspicions about their relationship drove her to confront Olson. She felt uncomfortable with Randy's hostile attitude and wanted him out of the house. Olson did not take well to this suggestion and proceeded to brutally rape his wife as a means to assert his terrifying and complete dominance over her. The next morning, she found the two men cuddling in their living room. Remembering her treatment the night before, she chose to ignore it.

One might wonder how someone so monstrously cruel could find any person to marry them. While Joan had a certain naivety about her, much of it was deliberate on her part. She learned quickly enough the kind of man that her husband was. When they first met, Olson had picked her and a friend up at a hotel bar. Olson initially was hoping to have sex with her friend, but at the end of the night, an unconsciously drunk Joan wound up in bed with him. A drunken one night stand was not typical for the previously divorced mother of two. The experience was both embarrassing and exciting. However, rather than remain a one-night stand, Olson continued to contact her. He loved to impress her with his grandiose tales and shower her with the kind of flattery and attention that she craved. Joan was smitten.

Whether Olson felt the same is highly unlikely. It is recognized that people with Antisocial Personality Disorder do not experience intimacy in the way that most functional people do. Their sense of love hinges on manipulating and controlling the other person in the relationship. He later admitted that the initial stage of their relationship was an opportunity for him to access her bank account and use her for convenient sex. However, he claimed to have eventually fallen in love with her. The circumstances of this revelation involved him blatantly cheating on Joan and convincing her to forgive him. He continued to flaunt his cheating throughout the rest of their marriage. It is unlikely that this scenario truly evoked feelings of love for Joan. More probable is that Olson felt satisfaction having tested Joan's limits and confirmed his ability to always be in control.

The Great Escape Artist

Olson only lasted two months on his parole before getting thrown back in jail. After he was caught doing break-ins, Olson went back to Oakalla with a new release date set for 1961. Incidentally, Olson's father was sent to the same prison shortly after Olson himself had left. His father was caught organizing a scam to get money from a local Bingo event. This scenario raises questions about what other kind of influences his father had on him. Along with the abuse, this kind of conniving behavior is something that Olson would have picked up and mimicked as a child. Olson felt these behaviors were innate to him. Perhaps his father had more influence than Olson realized or was willing to accept.

Another short three months out of prison in 1961, Olson was once again caught doing crimes and returned to Oakalla. It would seem as if he had absolutely no real desire to avoid prison. Many of his crimes were committed in the most risky way possible. He even made a second escape from prison by climbing over the yard fence during the middle of the day. In what became a pattern, Olson's crimes were often successful due to the incapability of the authorities to keep up with him.

After this second escape failed, Olson was sent to prison in Prince Albert, Saskatchewan. Almost immediately, he managed to escape once again by simply stealing some civilian clothes and walking right out of the prison in them. After only a few short hours, he was caught once again.

In the fall of 1962, Olson was released from prison in Prince Albert and went to Vancouver to join up with his prison husband, Lorne Johnson. The two of them went on a spree of stealing and conning until a few short months passed and he was once again arrested.

Olson stayed in and out of prison throughout the next few years with two other major escape attempts. In 1964, he was involved in an automobile accident while traveling the United States and left the scene before the cops could arrive. He was picked up by cops shortly after. While in custody, Olson manipulated his lawyer to let him go pick up bail money while unsupervised. He then headed for San Francisco and from there went back to New Westminster in B.C. with a teenage girl in tow.

Near the end of that summer, the RCMP had tracked Olson down to his parents' house where he was staying. They showed up at the house in the daytime and Olson made a run for it. A police dog named Rinty was later given Police Dog of the Year for managing to capture him.

His next major escape attempt was in 1965. He decided to start reporting the symptoms of a kidney disease to his doctor in prison. When the doctor requested a urine sample, Olson tampered with his sample by putting some of his own blood in it. Naturally, the results were concerning to the doctor. He was taken to an outside hospital for further testing, and the moment he was unsupervised, Olson made a dash for it. He was fortunate enough that this escape was relatively successful. He managed to evade police long enough to go commit more major crimes.

After leaving the hospital, Olson met up with a young man named Dave. Dave let

Olson stay with him and Olson let Dave join him on his crime sprees. They spent most of their time driving around and finding people to rob.

Olson eventually acquired a gun after robbing a house. Not wanting the gun to go to waste, he decided to put it to use one day. Olson and Dave were driving by a Safeway supermarket in Richmond, and Olson decided to rob it. He knew there would be thousands of dollars locked in the store safe. All he needed was an unsuspicious way to get into the office where the safe was stored.

He brought a large amount of groceries up to the cash register and tried to pay using a check. Olson knew that the check would require approval from management and so he followed the cashier into the manager's office. Once inside, he pulled out the gun and threatened the manager to give him the safe money. To his surprise, Olson was wrong about the location of the safe. It was actually in the front of the store. The manager led Olson to the front and unlocked the safe at gunpoint. However, in his anxiousness to get away before the police came, Olson grabbed the wrong bag of money. After all of his risky effort, they only made away with a total of $89.

A day later, the police had staked the pair out at Dave's house. Olson happened to notice a policeman's rifle on the roof of a neighbor's house. Olson alerted Dave and the two slipped out a side entrance and into Dave's car before the police noticed. They escaped to a cheap motel nearby and gleefully watched the press react to their exploits. Olson's mother commented in an interview, "This is the seventh time he's gotten away from the police. You've got to admit, he's quick on his feet." It was an unsurprising comment from a mother who had always indulged her child's misbehavior.

Throughout his criminal career, attention from the press was one of Olson's greatest pleasures. His first escape from prison had given him a taste for public attention. From that moment on, he was hooked on his ability to evoke reactions from the media. Doing so was an extension of his usual penchant for manipulation. The difference was that media attention was manipulation on a much grander scale. He reveled in the notion of being the most hated criminal in Canada, and it became a source of pride for him that he could repeatedly outsmart and antagonize the police. This aspect of his behavior was especially upsetting to the families of his victims. It was as if every time they could begin to forget about him, he made another appearance in the news for doing something bizarre.

In 2008, Olson tried to sell autographed photos, news clippings of himself, and legal documents on a website called murderauction.com. The items were starting at $1 - $7, and thankfully, no one made any bids. The uproar caused by this discovery led the Canadian Public Safety Minister, Stockwell Day, to make a public announcement condemning the website and the nature of its premise. He proposed to introduce legislation that would prohibit the ability for inmates to send personal items to people outside of prison. While they had the ability to do so, Corrections Canada did not decide to pursue the operator of the site to remove the items. Regarding the incident, the stepfather of the murdered Daryn Johnsrude, Gary Rosenfeldt, said, "You have to wonder what's next, is he going to have the hammer that he used to smash your son's head in?"

In the same year, a MySpace profile page appeared for Olson. It was unlikely that Olson himself was responsible for the page as inmates were not to have Internet access. However, Peter Worthington, a journalist who was close to Olson, said that Olson would scheme to acquire access to things he was prohibited from having. For example, Worthington would often receive phone calls from Olson even though Olson was prohibited from contacting members of the media. If the man can escape from prison that many times, it is not unbelievable to think he could also get Internet access while locked up. Most of the profiles befriended by Olson's MySpace page were for other notorious killers. There were some other very notable names amongst his friends list such as Frosty The Snowman and Madonna. While it is very unlikely that Olson would have made this page himself, the incident nonetheless brought his name back into the public's attention.

Road Trips With Evelyn and Glen

Spending so much time incarcerated had an interesting effect on Olson's learning. Prison is a natural setting to learn more about the criminal world for many people. In Olson's case, it was a perfect setting for him to study the world of the legal system. Despite having flunked in school, Olson was bright in his own way. He had a cunning personality, and if he felt he saw an opportunity to scheme, he would. This drove him to spend a significant amount of time and effort into researching and applying for his parole or filing complaints against people in the system for infringing on his rights.

Once, while incarcerated at the B.C. Penitentiary, Olson secretly broke into the chaplain's office. He then used a typewriter to alter a document relating to one of his charges. He increased his sentence from six months to two years so that he could later sue the prison for unlawful confinement. Fortunately, a thorough investigation found the tampering and dismissed Olson's charges.

Olson's numerous attempts at parole were also not very successful for him. In one scenario, Olson was caught engaging in a prison gang rape of a teenage inmate while awaiting a response to his application. Needless to say, he did not get his wish granted.

Finally, after eight years, Olson was released in August of 1972. Unsurprisingly, his typical behaviors of thievery, conning, and sexual relationships with minors commenced immediately. His parole officer at the time wrote, "I can see no possibility whatsoever that Olson would be able to function on the street. He is barely able to function in the institution." By this time, Olson had spent half of his life behind bars. It was hard to believe that anyone who had such a dysfunctional life could become a normal member of society.

By 1973, Olson was road tripping across Canada doing his usual spree of crime and mischief. It was during that August that he met a beautiful 20-year-old from Saskatchewan by the name of Evelyn Gagnon. He picked her up at a bus depot in

Saskatoon while he was traveling with a 14-year-old boy named Glen. Evelyn initially thought that Glen was supposed to be Olson's son. However, she quickly learned that was not the case and assumed that Glen had been homeless. She thought that Olson was just a nice guy who was helping Glen out of a tough situation.

Evelyn was impressed by Olson's honesty as he told her of his time spent imprisoned. Like most people, she gravitated to his smooth talking, cheerful persona. Against her better judgment, she began to trust Olson enough to willingly join him on a trip throughout Canada, with teenaged Glen in tow. The trio went all across Canada, zigzagging between different cities. From Saskatoon they went on to Edmonton, Calgary, Vancouver, Toronto, back to Vancouver, Victoria, Edmonton again, Hudson Bay, Calgary again, Winnipeg, Toronto again, Ottawa, Saskatoon again, Hudson Bay again, Winnipeg again, Thompson, Hudson Bay again, and then North Battleford.

Throughout the trip, Olson managed to have sexual relationships with both. He would leave them alone for periods of time while going out to do 'business'. While she seemed unfazed, Evelyn did notice the way that he would change his outfits and hairstyle before going out. They would always leave town shortly after business had been conducted. However, Olson forked over cash to Evelyn for whatever she wanted. She wasn't about to complain about his generosity.

By the beginning of September, the trio briefly went their separate ways. Evelyn reunited with an estranged boyfriend but quickly decided she preferred Olson's company. She ended up moving into the basement of Olson's sister, Sharon. Meanwhile Olson and Glen reunited in Toronto. After a short while, they decided to return to Vancouver to be with Evelyn and Sharon. The real reason they returned was because police had issued an indecent assault warrant for Olson having sex with Glen. Police continued to track Olson down, and this was when he and Evelyn went variously to Victoria, Edmonton, Hudson Bay, Calgary, Winnipeg, Toronto, and Ottawa. They were constantly evading the indecent assault warrants (there were now two pertaining to Glen), as well as the potential to get caught for thieving.

Eventually Olson and Evelyn made it to Hudson Bay to stay with Evelyn's family. He got along well with her family and charmed them much in the same way he charmed Evelyn. As they began to wear out their welcome, the two finally decided to leave. They spent a short amount of time traveling throughout Manitoba before returning to visit Evelyn's family in Hudson Bay.

During a moment alone, Evelyn's mother informed her that her Grandma had been robbed of all her savings. It was around the same time that Olson and Evelyn had previously left for Winnipeg. Olson was the main suspect as he had been spending a lot of time alone with the grandmother during their visit. Evelyn had also noticed that Olson had an influx of cash just after they had left. He told her it was money from his credit union and gave her $1,000 to use for herself. She was so used to accepting his stolen money, she did not consider that it could be from her own family.

The police had been notified and planned to investigate the matter. Evelyn agreed to spy on Olson while they continued on their travels. Finally, one day she decided to confront him while they were catching a bus away from North Battleford. Olson vehemently denied stealing from her grandmother's savings. At the next stop, Olson casually got off the bus but never returned.

The Rat Puts Away A Murderer

By the beginning of 1974, Olson was arrested again in Victoria and was sent to the B.C. Penitentiary. Typical of his efforts to gain parole, he enlisted the help of two women to try and get him released. The first was a young woman named Julie who claimed she was pregnant with his child and that they planned to marry. She pleaded on his behalf that becoming a father would kill his previous tendency to have sex with underage males.

The other young woman was named Stephanie. She had an almost identical story to Julie's. The difference was that Stephanie's child had already been born and she insisted that Olson was the father. Whether the women truly believed these stories is unclear. They may have just been trying to help him and realized it was a scam. Alternatively, Olson may have manipulated them to thinking that he truly wanted to fulfill these father figure roles. All he needed was the chance to prove it.

Regardless, the prison authorities were not taken in by these sob stories. Perhaps their identical content killed the sympathy that such tales were supposed to generate. They were convinced that Olson was homosexual as opposed to acknowledging his preferences as being more bisexual. They did not believe his relationships with these women could be genuine on his part.

Shortly after, Olson was transferred to the Saskatchewan Penitentiary where his assassination attempt occurred. After the assassination attempt, most of the participants were given charges for attempted murder. Two of the men involved were unable to be identified by Olson. Their charges could not be pursued. With his skills in working the system, Olson translated this event into an opportunity to milk money wherever he could. He applied to the Saskatchewan Criminal Injuries Compensation Board and received $3,500.

Lussier had later stated that the impetus for the murder was because Olson was a rapist. However, it is also known that at least part of the murder attempt was driven by Olson's reputation as an informant. As such, the authorities felt some responsibility for Olson as he had been stabbed doing work on their behalf. Olson said of the incident, "...I was trying to be a good citizen, and get rid of drugs. I had a duty to help. The money was kind of recognition of this."

Ironically, Olson's next major work as an informant was to gain a confession from a fellow child rapist and murderer named Gary Marcoux. It was 1976 and Marcoux was being investigated for the murder of a nine-year-old named Jeanne Dove. He was placed in a cell close to Olson at the B.C. Penitentiary. It was not long before Olson made an effort to befriend Marcoux.

They discussed his case and Marcoux assured Olson that the police had nothing to pin on him for Dove's murder. Eventually Marcoux approached Olson to help give him an alibi for his whereabouts on the night of the murder. He wanted Olson to say that they had been smoking marijuana together on the night that Dove was killed.

Olson agreed to help Marcoux, but he had one stipulation. He made Marcoux write out every iota of detail regarding the alibi he wished to concoct. A few days after receiving Marcoux's handwritten details regarding the alibi, Olson wrote a letter to the Attorney General of British Columbia enclosing the information he collected. From that point on, Olson kept a detailed journal of all his interactions with Marcoux. Eventually Olson managed to get exactly what he wanted. Marcoux confessed both in writing and verbally the exact details of how he murdered Jeanne Dove. This was Olson the manipulator at his finest.

That December, Olson signed an affidavit stating that the alibi was in fact true. Less than a month later, he signed another affidavit detailing the alibi as a fabrication. He then divulged the specifics of Dove's murder as told to him by Marcoux.

A lawyer by the name of Bob Shantz was suddenly very relieved. He had spent so much time stressing over how in the world he was going to prosecute Dove's murderer without the solid evidence required. Marcoux had completely ruined his own case by trusting Olson. He admitted his guilt and was given 25 years with no parole. Shantz was impressed by Olson's meticulousness in extracting this confession. Olson himself never forgot about Shantz. When the time came, it was no coincidence that Shantz became Olson's own lawyer.

Poor, Poor Debbie

While Olson's criminal life was marked by his antisocial characteristics, lack of understanding of his deeper issues made his later behaviors surprising to the authorities. To the public reading about his life, it seemed like he should have been such an obvious and immediate suspect for the spree of murders that he carried out. However, his ability to charm and be goofy made him seem more harmless than he truly was. If anything could serve as a precursory indication to his more volatile nature, it was his relationship with a 23-year-old woman named Debbie.

Olson picked up Debbie as she was hitchhiking to B.C. from Alberta in February of 1977. Debbie was a bit of a hippie type with a laid back, free spirited demeanor. As Olson rode passenger down the Trans Canada Highway with a man named John, he spotted Debbie. He was immediately interested and called out for her to come catch a ride. Debbie was already high on acid when Olson gave her a beer.

At the time he picked up Debbie, Olson was actually on his way to meet up with Stephanie, the girl who claimed he was the father of her child. That night, Olson and Debbie stayed in a motel in Keremos. By this point, Debbie was additionally intoxicated from some sleeping pills that Olson had been prescribed in prison. Unable to give consent, Debbie did not remember getting raped by Olson that night. As always, Olson did not care about the well-being of his sexual partners. He was not bothered at all by Debbie's unconsciousness.

The following day, Olson and Debbie went to a hotel in Abbotsford where Stephanie was to come meet him. Naturally, she was not pleased to find Olson with another woman. Despite her disdain for Debbie, Stephanie still shared a bed with the two of them. Olson had sex with both women separately and tried to convince Stephanie that he was truly in love with her. She gave up trying to make him monogamous and decided to leave Olson with Debbie. It was probably one of the best decisions she ever made.

As for Debbie, her routine with Olson quickly became very negative. He constantly forced her to take sleeping pills in order to keep her disoriented. He aggressively raped her whenever he felt the need. It seemed as though she had become involved with a nightmare of an abusive boyfriend. In her drugged-up and miserable state, Debbie was far too scared to try and leave Olson.

One day, things reached a boiling point and Debbie bravely tried to make an escape. Earlier that day, Olson had made Debbie shave her entire body so that she would seem more childlike. He then raped her several times and forced her to let him bathe her. Things escalated to the point where he held her head under the water long enough that she began to think he was trying to kill her. He then abruptly let go of her head and went into another room. Debbie tried to break out of a window in the motel, but Olson noticed her. He clutched at her and forced her back inside as a car passed by. Olson began to beat Debbie and threatened her with a knife. Later that night, he forced her to repeat the bath ritual before drugging her once again. It was then that Debbie realized she was completely imprisoned.

When they caught a cab the next day, Olson began hitting Debbie when she tried to escape. He convinced the cab driver that she was his daughter and that he was simply disciplining her for being a drug user. The cab driver was very sympathetic.

On another day, Olson took Debbie to meet his sister Sharon and her male friend at a bar. For some reason, Debbie was unaware that the two were siblings. Once in private, Sharon warned Debbie that she should stop dating Olson. Sharon was clearly oblivious that the relationship had surpassed the point where Debbie could simply leave. Later that night, the two ended up on Sharon's doorstep. Debbie was given a room to sleep alone, but in the morning, Olson sneaked in through the window and raped her.

What followed was a very bizarre period of time in which Olson's sister was complicit in imprisoning Debbie. Despite having been a victim of Olson's sexual abuse herself, Sharon enabled Olson to keep Debbie from escaping. Sharon did show some concern for Debbie and asked privately if Olson had been hurting her. However, Sharon was also too terrified to defy her brother. Debbie suspected that Olson and Sharon were having sex with each other during this stay.

Feeling empathy for the girl, Sharon offered to take Debbie to a doctor. For some inexplicable reason, this doctor simply prescribed Debbie some tranquilizers as opposed to alerting police that she was being kept against her will. Debbie eventually made the smart move of only pretending to take the various medications being forced upon her. She would put them in her mouth and then secretly throw them out when no one was watching.

Sharon's guilt caught up with her and she finally enlisted the help of a social services agency. The agency put Debbie in the care of a highly religious German couple named Gisela and Gunter Kleinschmidt. Debbie's new location was supposed to be kept confidential by the agency. However, Sharon did not want to seem defiant so she gave Olson the name of the agency and pleaded ignorance to Debbie's whereabouts. It only took a matter of minutes before Olson convinced the secretary at the agency to give him that information.

Olson went over to the Kleinschmidts and not only convinced them to let him see Debbie, but also convinced them to let him move into their house and give him a job. As Debbie was very withdrawn after being medicated and abused, the Kleinschmidts were much less attracted to her than they were to Olson. For his part, Olson created a persona in which he was a wayward soul who had come back to love and devote himself to the Lord. With their trust invested in Olson rather than Debbie, the Kleinschmidts naively continued the cycle of imprisonment that Debbie had come into. They continued to medicate her under the direction of a new doctor, and Debbie continued to only pretend to take the pills. And of course, Olson continued to rape and abuse Debbie outside of the Kleinschmidts' awareness.

Finally, the stress of living with Olson caused Debbie to completely snap. While attending service at the Kleinschmidts' church, Debbie began to have outbursts declaring she was having hallucinations of Satan and God speaking to her. This happened enough times that the church congregation began to simply ignore her.

Another night, she managed to sneak out of the house with the Kleinschmidts' dog, Timber. Debbie was wearing nothing but a bathrobe and she went around the neighborhood trying to get the help she so desperately needed. Unfortunately, her extreme level of stress made her appear psychotic and so no one trusted her belief that she was under grave threat of being killed. Some of the neighbors phoned the police, as did Gisela Kleinschmidt when she noticed Debbie had snuck out of the house. Debbie was returned to the Kleinschmidts' house and had blacked out the memory by the time she awoke the next day.

A few days later, Debbie finally escaped. She was at a mall in Surrey while under the surveillance of Gisela, Sharon, and their friend. Debbie decided to make a run for it and pushed Sharon out of her way. She ran towards the street as the women chased her. In a wonderful stroke of fortune, Debbie managed to catch the attention of a truck driver. She quickly told him that the women chasing her were trying to kidnap her. The driver took pity and sped away with Debbie as his passenger.

While Debbie was lucky to escape Olson's murderous streak, she was forever scarred by those six weeks. Debbie displayed signs of post traumatic stress disorder and sought psychiatric help to cope with the ordeal. She was living in Calgary when she suddenly panicked one day thinking that she saw Olson. She immediately quit her job and moved away to Nova Scotia. Shortly after, Debbie spent five years in a psychiatric institution.

This situation was a perfect reflection of Olson's unbelievable ability to dominate others. This scenario did not happen because Debbie was weak or irresponsible. Olson broke her sense of independence through physical and mental abuse. Despite this, Debbie tried as hard as she could to escape Olson's control. She made numerous attempts to thwart his influence by either trying to flee or secretly rejecting the drugs forced upon her. And yet, it took far too long for one of these attempts to be successful. This was largely because of the compliance of Sharon and the Kleinschmidts, coupled with the dismissiveness of the police, neighbors, and medical professionals she encountered. It demonstrates the systematic and deliberate way in which Olson would manage to entrap his victims.

After the incident with Debbie, Olson returned to prison. However, he kept a close relationship with the Kleinschmidts by maintaining his religious façade. He took Bible courses and tried to use his newly found religiosity to ask for parole. By the beginning of 1978, he was living once more with the couple and using a job with Gunter's construction company as a cover for scams. After a few weeks, he was again in and out of prison and running from police. This cat-and-mouse chase took Olson traveling all over Canada and into the United States. He then returned to prison and was not released until 1980.

That was the year he met Joan. After meeting her that night at the bar, Olson sought out Joan at her work the next day. He moved in with her four days later. Joan would do anything Olson asked of her. This included handing over any money that she had and even letting Olson take naked pictures of her and her children.

It didn't take long for their marriage to turn abusive. Joan learned quickly not to bother Olson about his negative behaviors such as bringing home young boys or drinking and driving. One night he broke Joan's nose because she asked him not to drink and drive. Years later while testifying in court, Joan said, "My husband was an alcoholic, and I was very scared of him. He was an animal. He terrorized me, he scared me, he beat me." Much like with Debbie, Joan was subjected to his abuse on a daily basis. Unlike Debbie, Joan did not have the same courage to leave Olson until after he was arrested for the murders. The abuse was terrifying, and she clung to the moments in which he would return to being the charming and doting man she had initially fallen for.

In the summer of 1980, Olson decided to take Joan to visit the B.C. Penitentiary where he had spent so much of his time. The prison was closing down and he wanted to show it off to his wife. Unbeknownst to him, his mandatory release had been retracted and police were once again looking for him. After being recognized by a guard, Olson was arrested on the spot, and instead taken to prison in New Westminster. Olson was released in June, and a month later Joan was pregnant with his child.

The First Victim

Monday, November 17, 1980. Christine Anne Weller dropped her father off at the Surrey Inn while he had a beer before supper. Twelve-year-old Christine had just borrowed a bike from a friend named Clive Walker. She was riding it around nearby the inn as she waited for her father to finish.

The same night, Olson had been fighting with Joan. He had come home from a long day of thieving only to find an angry note in which she accused him of only loving "drink, sex, and boys". Most likely, the note was inspired by the violence he had inflicted on her the previous day. Olson decided his best course of action was to continue drinking and go out searching for his pregnant wife. Before he made any progress, however, someone else caught his eye.

Olson noticed Christine along the King George Highway. He drove up beside her bike and inquired about the location of the local unemployment office. He quickly sussed her out through a short series of questions. Olson knew her age; he knew that she didn't have a boyfriend; he knew that she was waiting for her father at the bar; he knew she was from a dysfunctional family; and he knew that no one would be looking for her immediately.

Olson decided to take the opportunity. He showed her a few of his tacky business cards and offered Christine a job washing windows. He told her that he paid $10 per hour. It was an exciting prospect for a young girl used to living in poverty. He offered her a beer and insisted she leave her bike to come catch a ride with him in his car. Olson did his best to keep Christine calm while in his presence. Knowing that she had already mentioned she did not see her mother regularly, Olson made a point of saying he wanted to speak with her mother. Hearing that he wanted to talk to her parents made Christine feel somewhat more comfortable.

Olson drove Christine to a house that was being built by Gunter's construction company under the pretense that he had to pick up another employee. He told

Christine to have some more beers while they toured the house and waited for the other girl to arrive. Olson talked to Christine about her upbringing and her life at school. He assessed that she was a rather solitary person and vulnerable to kindness and attention. After he had fed her several drinks, Olson made a move on Christine and began to make out with her. He would have raped her if he had not already ejaculated in his pants a few minutes into fooling around. When he finished, he told her he had to go pick up some marijuana. It was now several hours after Christine had planned to be home. However, Olson had promised her some of this weed for free. She did not protest.

In actuality, Olson was driving back to his own apartment to see if Joan had returned. He told Christine to stay in the car while he went upstairs. Joan was still out. Olson grabbed his bottle of sleeping pills and decided to find somewhere safer to take Christine. As he was leaving, the building's security guard asked him about the young girl in his car. Olson assured the guard that the young girl was actually his niece. The security guard was likely unfamiliar with the fact that Olson had been arrested several times as a child molester. If only he had, he may have been able to save Christine's life.

Back in the car, Olson convinced Christine to take some of his sleeping pills. He told her that they were "wake-up pills" and pretended to take some himself. They began to drive down the highway, stopping only at a Denny's to get some take-out. By now, Christine was barely conscious. Olson parked the car in a field and raped Christine a few times before leaving her to continue sleeping in the field. He was not sure what his next move should be. Olson decided that regardless of Joan, he would take Christine back to the house with him. He had done it several times before and was not concerned about Joan's reaction.

Olson tried to drive away but the car got stuck in the mud of the field. After an hour of trying to get the vehicle moving, he decided it was hopeless. He needed a tow truck to come. However, he also could not afford to have someone find Christine drugged and passed out in his car. He decided he would have to drown her before he could get a tow truck to come. Olson woke Christine up and told her they had to start walking since the car was stuck. They began walking towards the river. Christine could hardly stand and held on to Olson for support. After she passed out in the middle of the walk, he took her back to the car and tried to get it started again. He also raped Christine another time before strangling her with her own shoelaces. He gripped the laces so hard that they eventually broke. Somehow, Christine still managed to breathe. Olson took out a hunting knife and stabbed Christine twice in the heart and slit across her throat.

He cried as he buried her body in the thicket of blackberry bushes. He threw the knife and all of Christine's belongings into the Fraser River. Anything that could be used to properly identify the body was burned. The only things that didn't make it to the river were a crucifix necklace and a ring she had been wearing. He cleaned up the car and changed his own clothes. By now, it was four in the morning. Olson went to a hotel and called an all-night towing service. When he finally made it back to the apartment, Joan had still not returned. Olson burned the clothes he had been wearing when he murdered Christine and called his mother's house.

The next day, Olson drove to the U.S. and stayed at the Holiday Inn under the names of Mr. and Mrs. Olson. He felt confident with his alibi. He then drove to Coquitlam to reunite with Joan and then took her back to Bellingham for a nice vacation. It was a perfectly relaxing getaway to forget the fact that he had just committed murder.

In the meantime, the only people looking for Christine at this point were Clive and Alex Walker. Clive was the friend that had lent Christine the bike on the night that she had disappeared. Alex was his angry father. Both were worried that the penniless young girl had opted to steal Clive's bike. Alex was not about to let that happen and set out on November 24 to get it back.

They visited the Bonanza Hotel where Christine usually lived with her grandmother. Christine's grandmother was not particularly concerned that her granddaughter had been missing for a few days. She had run away on previous occasions. Frustrated with the grandmother's indifferent attitude, Alex phoned the police and tried to file a missing person report. The police advised him to contact the Welfare Crisis Center as only relatives could file missing person reports. The Crisis Center was equally unconcerned. They knew she was a runaway and figured she was probably just staying with a friend. Over the next month, Alex tried numerous times and avenues to try and raise awareness that Christine was missing. His concern was no longer simply about the bike. He was genuinely worried about the whereabouts of the missing young girl whom no one seemed to care about.

It was not until Christmas day of 1980 that Christine's body was found by a man out for a walk. An RCMP serious crimes investigator, Fred Maile, came to the scene the following day. Maile was to be a key player investigating the other murders that Olson was about to commit. However, the immediate suspects were Clive Walker and Christine's father, Richard. The police did speak with the owner of the hotel from which Olson had called the tow truck. However, they were inquiring about the wrong date since Christine's grandmother was not actually sure when the girl went missing. After Richard and Clive were eliminated, another suspect emerged. He was a man who lived at the same hotel as Christine's grandmother. Christine and the man had previously had sex and so her DNA was present in his apartment. The police did not have quite enough evidence to formally charge him, but they locked into him as the suspect. They did not bother to look elsewhere.

That New Year's Eve, Olson got drunk and confessed to a group of people that he had raped and stabbed a young girl to death. He then elaborated that, in fact, someone else had killed Christine Weller. Olson told the crowd he could not name the murderer because they would seek revenge and kill him. The conversation was making the guests at the party uncomfortable. Joan repeatedly told Olson to stop talking. However, no one took his claims seriously. A person would have to be insane to confess to being a murderer in that kind of setting. They thought he was tastelessly bullshitting them.

Kim and Colleen Meet Olson

Only a week after Christine's body was found, Olson picked up a 16-year-old named Kim Werbecky. Olson gave Kim a job offer in Whistler and access to his large supply of beer. They headed up to Squamish. Upon arrival, Olson got into a fight with some local people in which he ended up firing a gun at them. Olson then raped Kim at a local motel as well as on the drive back to Vancouver. They stopped at a gas station and Kim ran and hid in the bathroom until he finally left. After the ordeal, Kim went to police to get rape and indecent assault charges against Olson. He was also given charges of committing two firearms offenses because the fight in Squamish had been reported.

Olson was arrested without bail and held for three months. He decided to contact Bob Shantz, the lawyer who had prosecuted Gary Marcoux. As Olson's interference in that case had been so crucial to convicting Marcoux, Shantz agreed to represent him. From then on, Shantz remained as Olson's lawyer.

Unfortunately, Kim had to drop the rape charges when it came to light that she had previously been a sex worker. During the initial court date for the weapons charges, Shantz interrogated her in a demeaning and intimidating manner. He even asked her if she had mistaken a "pencil" for a gun. Kim did not show up at their next court date. She accurately assumed that the bias against her would discredit her testimony. Commenting on the case in 1994, Kim told reporters, "If a British Columbia Crown Counsel had not decided a former child prostitute could not be raped, Clifford Olson would have been in jail and not killed the ten children he did in the four months after he raped me. There is a government lawyer who must be suffering, and the guilt belongs to him, not me. It's not my fault I survived and the Crown's lawyer wouldn't even talk to me."

Olson was free to go by April of 1981. A short while later, his son Stephen was born. During the period that Joan was staying in the hospital, Olson took the opportunity to rape several other young children.

One of these children was 13-year-old Colleen Daignault. Much like Christine, she mostly lived with her grandmother and sometimes with her father. She also had a lot of independence afforded by her unstable upbringing. On the night of April 15, 1981, Olson noticed Colleen skateboarding home from visiting with a friend.

Olson drove up beside her and used the same spiel he had used on Christine. He wanted to know where the unemployment office was so that he could advertise that he was looking to hire young girls to wash windows. He immediately began giving her beers and tricking her into taking the sleeping pills. After raping Colleen, Olson tried to kill her by pumping air into her vein with a hypodermic needle that he had stolen from his doctor. Since he wasn't able to locate an artery, the exercise did nothing and he threw out the needle.

Olson drove to a secluded spot along the drive to Surrey. Feeling safe in their secluded, forested spot, Olson fell asleep. When he woke up the next day, he decided that his initial impulse to kill Colleen was the correct course of action. After raping her once more, Olson made Colleen begin the walk away from the car and into the woods. He told her they were going to visit a house that he had built. When they finally reached an ideal stop, Olson asked Colleen to reach up into a tree to grab a key that he had hidden there. With her back turned to Olson, she did not notice him bring out the hammer he had secretly brought with him. He hit her in the back of the head and broke her skull. Colleen began to bleed profusely. Olson removed her clothes and buried them nearby. He left the body in the woods and covered it somewhat with leaves and tree branches.

Olson then drove to meet Joan at the hospital where he was to pick up her and the baby. When he arrived late, Joan immediately noticed the blood on his clothes. Not wanting to provoke a fight, she did not bother to ask what it was from.

Almost a week later, Colleen's grandmother reported that she was missing. Unlike with Christine, her family did not suspect she had run away. Her grandmother, Julie White, merely thought that Colleen had been staying with a friend. She had been a happy girl. No one close to her believed there would be a reason for her to run away from home. However, the police suspected that perhaps she had run away to find her mother. After some effort, the RCMP was able to contact Colleen's mother. She said she had no knowledge of her daughter's whereabouts. With police indifference, the investigation was at a standstill.

Photos

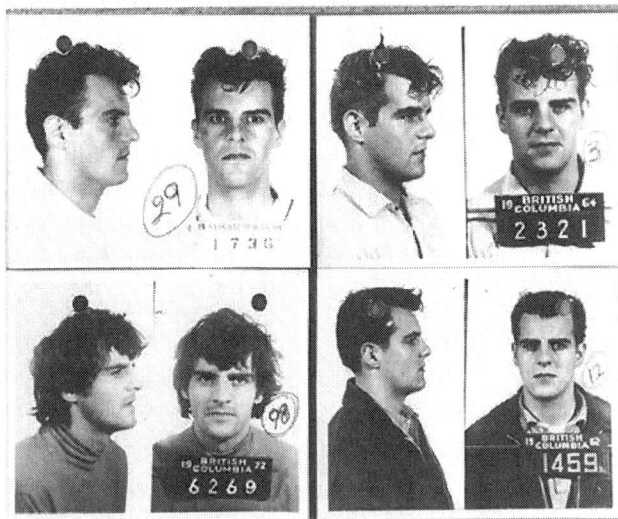

Mugshots of Olson over time

Olson in shackles going to court

Olson going to hospital where he died of cancer

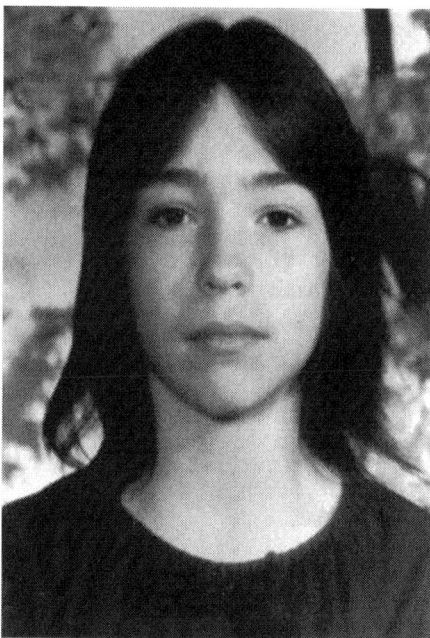

Victim # 1 ~ Christine Weller, 12

Olson's first victim, 12-year-old Christine Weller disappeared on Nov. 17, 1980, while riding her bike home in Surrey, B.C. Initially, police didn't treat her death as suspicious. Her body, which was stabbed and showed signs of strangulation, was found along Fraser River dikes in nearby Richmond on Christmas Day.

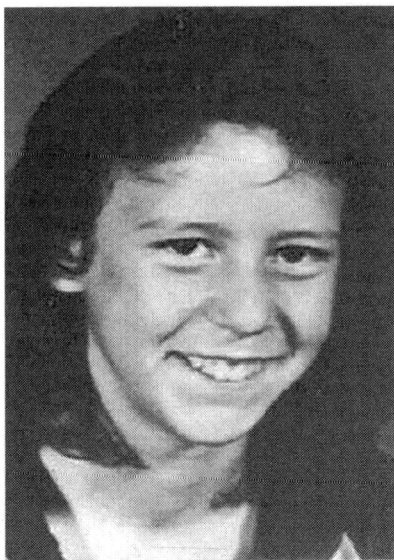

Victim # 2 ~ Colleen Marian Daignault, 13

Colleen Daignault of Surrey, B.C., was 13 when she disappeared on April 16, 1981. She was raped and murdered before her body was dumped in isolated woods, where it was found five months later.

Victim # 3 ~ Daryn Todd Johnsrude, 16

Daryn Johnsrude, 16, had been in Vancouver for two days on a visit from Saskatoon when he disappeared from a local mall on April 21, 1981. His body was found less than two weeks later on May 2.

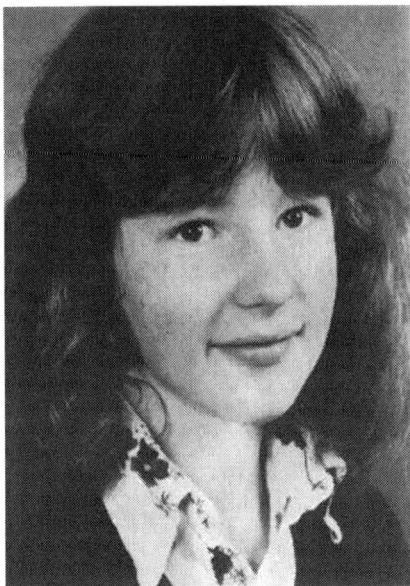

Victim # 4 ~ Sandra Wolfsteiner, 16

Sandra Wolfsteiner was hitchhiking from her boyfriend's home on May 19, 1981, when Olson picked up the 16-year-old and offered her a window-cleaning job. Her remains were found several weeks later in the Fraser Valley bush.

Victim # 5 ~ Ada Anita Court, 13

Thirteen-year-old Ada Court disappeared on June 21, 1981, while waiting for a bus after a babysitting job in the same apartment complex where Olson lived. Her body was found two months later. A logging camp chef interrupted Olson disposing of the body.

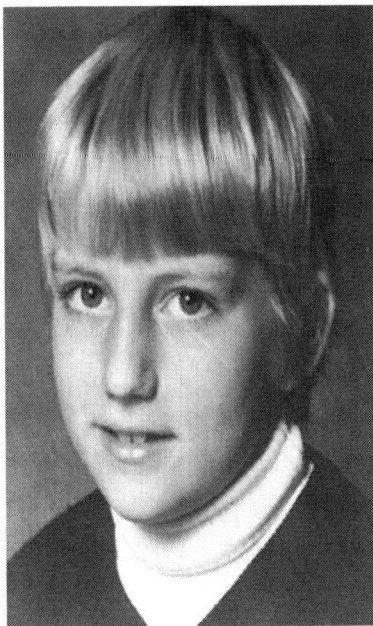

Victim # 6 ~ Simon Partington, 9

Simon Partington, 9, of Surrey,B.C., disappeared July 2, 1981, while riding his bike to a friend's home. Police had classified previous disappearances as runaways, but admitted Simon was the victim of foul play.

Victim # 7 ~ Judy Kozma, 14

Olson abducted 14-year-old Judy Kozma on July 9, 1981, and plied her with liquor and drugs before killing her. Her body was found in a wooded area on July 25.

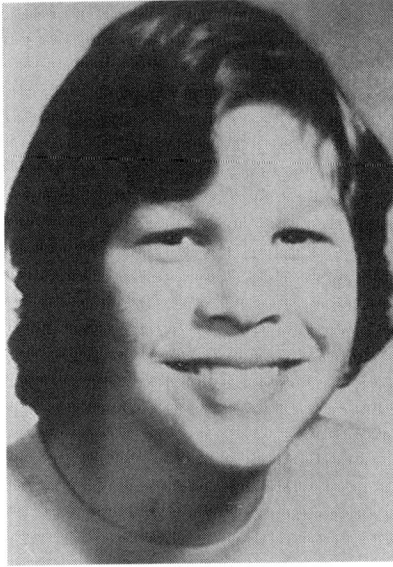

Victim # 8 ~ Raymond King Jr., 15

Raymond King Jr., 15, was at a bus stop on July 23, 1981, when Olson lured him away with the promise of work. Olson brutally beat King and dumped his body in a remote camping ground.

Victim # 9 ~ Sigrun Arnd, 18

Sigrun Arnd was an 18-year-old student visiting from Germany when she disappeared on July 25, 1981. Her disappearance wasn't noted until Olson eventually confessed. Olson cashed Arnd's travelers checks two days later at a bank in Hope, the same day he killed another teenage girl.

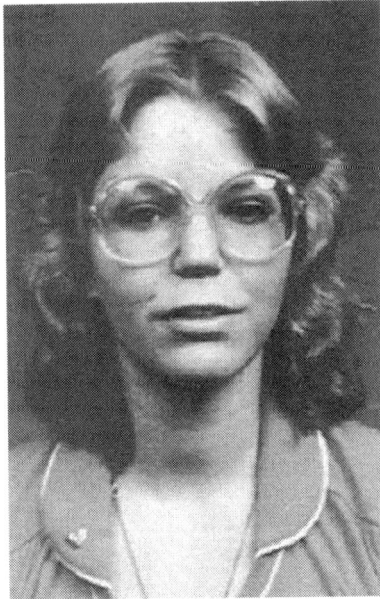

Victim # 10 ~ Terri Lyn Carson, 15

Terri Lyn Carson, 15, disappeared on July 27, 1981. Olson drugged, raped and strangled her before abandoning her body in a wooded area along the Fraser River.

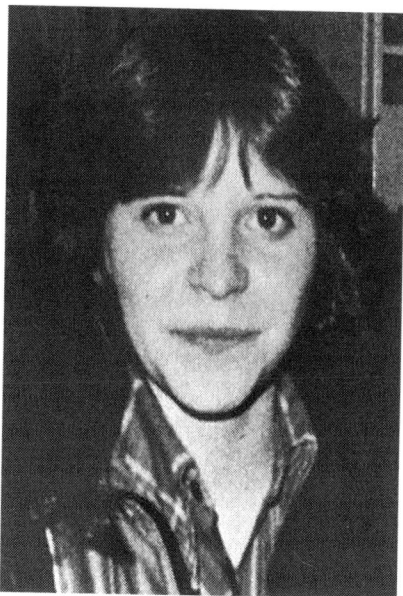

Victim # 11 ~ Louise Chartrand, 17

Olson abducted 17-year-old Louise Marie Chartrand on July 30, 1981, while she was on her way to a night job as a waitress. Olson drove her to an area near Whistler, B.C., and killed her before burying her body in a shallow grave. Hours earlier, RCMP investigators met with Olson and offered him cash to act as an informant to help with unsolved murders.

Daryn Disappears

On April 21, 1981, the same night that Colleen was reported missing, Daryn Johnsrude met Clifford Olson. Daryn was visiting Coquitlam from Saskatoon to stay with his mother and stepfather over Easter break. The 16-year-old was walking to buy cigarettes when Olson noticed him. Once again, Olson used the job offer as bait to get him in the car. Daryn was immediately excited when Olson insisted that the job entailed a lot of smoking marijuana and drinking beer. He began his routine with the beer and the sleeping pills until Daryn was sufficiently intoxicated.

Olson took the car off of the highway to the north of the Fraser River down to a more secluded, forested area. He raped Daryn while he lay unconscious on a picnic blanket. Olson took Daryn for a short walk before striking him with the hammer several times and killing him. He then threw the murder weapon and Daryn's clothing into the Fraser River. Much like when he murdered Christine, Olson's car got stuck trying to escape. He paid a young man to tow him out of two separate ditches on the way out. Later that night after getting his car cleaned, Olson was arrested for driving under the influence.

It was this night that Joan later remembered as very suspicious. Olson was at his parents' house and drunkenly phoned Joan. Both Olson and his parents were audibly crying. Joan was not sure what to make of it. Joan demanded to speak with his mother and asked why they were all crying. His mother responded, "I can't tell you, Clifford made me promise not to tell anyone." Despite asking several times over the years what Olson had told them that night, his parents would never tell. Their responses were always highly emotional. Joan even caught Olson burning his clothes and shoes from the day of the murder. He told her to mind her own business.

Meanwhile, Daryn's mother and stepfather were very concerned. His stepfather, Gary Rosenfeldt, later became a major advocate for victim's rights in Canada after their poor experience of dealing with the police. Gary was surprised and disappointed at the lack of concern when the police came to interview them. Daryn was 16 and had a history of behavioral problems. Naturally, he had to be a runaway. Knowing the police weren't looking, Gary spent his time searching throughout the streets of Vancouver. He was hoping to spot Daryn amongst the groups of homeless youth living there.

On May 2, two men out walking their dogs found Daryn's body draped over a tree stump. His face was so decomposed and destroyed from the hammer that he could only be identified through dental records. The police contacted the Rosenfeldts and told them that a body had been found and that the medical examination proved it was not Daryn. A few days later, the RCMP called again. "Mrs. Rosenfeldt, I'm sorry, I guess it was your boy after all." This horrifying blunder made an already devastating experience much worse.

Fred Maile was once again called in to investigate the scene. As the body was so decomposed, there was not much he could surmise about the motive for the killing. He figured it was a homosexual relationship that had ended badly. However, he still had to investigate Daryn's parents first. He found out that Daryn and his stepfather had fought several times over Daryn's drug use. Daryn had much of the angst of a typical teen combined with the stress of divorced parents. The notion that it may have been the parents or a lover began to dissipate.

Interestingly, Olson's name was on the list of suspects. Because he had a criminal record and lived in the area, it was automatically added. However, Colleen's body had not been found, and so the connection of the hammer as the murder weapon was not yet made. Furthermore, the different sexes of Christine Weller and Daryn Johnsrude complicated things. Both were young people with troubled backgrounds, but a bisexual serial killer was not a common scenario. It did not seem like a logical connection at the time.

How He Almost Got Caught

On May 19, 1981, Olson picked up a 16-year-old girl named Sandra Lynn Wolfsteiner. Sandra was hitchhiking when Olson noticed her. That day she was off to meet her 22-year-old boyfriend for lunch. After talking for a short while, Olson found that Sandra was unemployed. He offered Sandra a job and a cheap price on a luxury apartment in a building he owned. He also offered to help her buy a vehicle so that she could move in that weekend. Sandra could not believe how lucky she was. She and Olson drove to a bank and Sandra pretended to withdraw the $1,000 that she had saved up. He said that he would use the money to buy the car for her since he would likely get a better deal.

As they began driving towards Cultus Lake, Olson spoke adoringly of his beautiful new wife, Joan. Sandra felt assured that he wasn't a creep. He told her they were going to pick up some construction tools in the area. Sandra drank several beers and took the sleeping pills he offered. She was on the clock now, and getting paid to drink beer seemed like a great deal.

Once they parked, Olson told Sandra to start walking up the trail towards the nonexistent cabin. After a short while of walking, Olson brought the hammer out and began beating Sandra with it. He raped her when she was almost dead before leaving her body covered in branches and leaves. Even though she was still breathing, he knew it wouldn't be long before she lost that ability. Olson changed clothes and then threw her belongings and the hammer out as he drove away from the scene.

Sandra's boyfriend, Keith, was alarmed that she never showed up for their lunch. After calling her mother and confirming that Sandra had planned to meet him, Keith called the police. However, they told him that he could only file a missing person report once two days had passed. Even once her father filed the report, police assumed Sandra had merely run away.

In the meantime, Olson was continuing to have run-ins over incidents of sexual harassment towards young girls.

One very chilling incident involved a girl named Kathy Sallow. On May 26, he picked up the 15-year-old while she was hanging around outside of a convenience store. It was a few short blocks away from where Olson had recently picked up Daryn. Kathy had dropped out of school, and so Olson had an immediate in for offering her the job. Despite feeling uncomfortable, Kathy drank four beers and took three of the four sleeping pills that Olson gave to her. Everything was unfolding as it normally did. Olson had begun to fondle Kathy when he suddenly crashed the car. The car flipped over onto its roof.

A small group of construction workers noticed the crash and came to help. When Olson asked them to call for help but emphasized not to call police, Spud Dyer was immediately suspicious. He was not sure if it was just the effects of the crash disorienting her; but Dyer could not help but notice the intoxicated young girl who was with the middle-aged man. Dyer phoned his friend at a tow trucking company, knowing that his friend would call police on his own anyway.

Dyer gave the two a lift to the towing station. Olson spotted the police driving by and immediately freaked out. He grabbed Kathy and began running towards a nearby high school. Dyer sent the police in the direction of the school to chase after him. Olson ran into the office of the school and demanded that they immediately call a taxi for him. Alarmed at his urgency, the receptionist panicked and called for a taxi before notifying the vice principal about the strange man aggressively pulling a young girl around.

Feeling agitated, Olson ran out of the office and entered the school library against the protestations of the librarian. The school's vice principal caught up with them and demanded to know what was going on. Olson gave the vice principal several different names before finally explaining that his car had been overturned. As soon as Olson left the school, the principal told the receptionist to cancel the taxi and instead call the police.

When the police arrived, Olson backtracked through the school. The chase continued throughout the high school grounds, with the RCMP officer unable to catch up with him. Finally, Olson dumped Kathy's barely conscious body and escaped on his own.

The RCMP officer later found Olson at a nearby taxi stand with blood on his shirt. He confronted Olson about Kathy but Olson claimed he had never seen her before. Kathy, was so out of it, she was unable to speak up and immediately incriminate Olson. Olson gave the officer his real identification and fled while his criminal record check was being run. The police caught up with him shortly after, and Olson was arrested for impaired driving and contributing to juvenile delinquency. Olson promised to show up for court and they let him go. Kathy was incredibly lucky for that car crash.

The officer who responded and saved Kathy's life was a man named Darryll Kettles. Kettles noted that Kathy was picked up in very close proximity to where Daryn Johnsrude was seen last. Not having enough evidence to warrant investigating Olson for Daryn's murder, Kettles was forced to let Olson go. He knew that Olson was not going to show up for court, and he also knew that he had found the man responsible for the spate of child murders that had occurred that summer.

The following day, Kettles received a call from Kathy's mother, who had an unlisted number. Olson had called their house to say that Kathy still had a job offer and that he would come pick her up from the house if she still wanted the job. Kathy's mother was appalled. Kettles was determined to make a case for Olson. He immediately contacted Maile about the matter.

Unfortunately, Kettle's persistence that Olson was the killer fell on deaf ears. The RCMP is a highly bureaucratic and hierarchical organization. Kettles did not have the rank to have his ideas taken seriously despite their legitimacy. When he did call Maile, Maile gave him a dismissive comment before hanging up the phone on him.

Maile later described the incident somewhat differently. He said that Kettles was extremely emotional but could not provide the solid evidence necessary to pursue someone as a suspect. Regardless, the disorganization amongst various factions of the RCMP meant key information was often left out in communication. Kettles tried his best to get access to a meeting in July regarding the murders but was denied. Years later, Kettles spoke bitterly about the ordeal. He felt that if he had been able to have his voice heard, the rest of the murders would not have occurred.

Kathy wasn't the only close call for Olson during that time. In another instance, Olson was accused of molesting a toddler that he had been babysitting. Olson defended himself to the cops that he had simply been putting some cream on a vaginal rash she was having. Shortly after, he was once again investigated for drugging and raping a young teen named Sharon. There was no car crash to save her, but for some reason, Olson decided not to kill Sharon. The circumstances were almost exactly the same as when he did commit murder. Despite always being prepared with the necessary tools to do it, Olson's impulse to kill was quite random. He had raped and drugged several youths over the years, but he only killed some.

Sharon reported Olson to the police. However, since she did not press formal charges, he was let go. Again, it seems logical to consider the rape and murder of two young teens should be connected to Olson. He was a local man with an extensive criminal record and a recent history of similar rape accusations against children. He was even a suspect in one of the murders. Yet, he still went about freely.

A Killing Spree

June 21, 1981, 13-year-old Ada Court was walking home to Burnaby when Olson offered her a ride. Since she was heading home in order to go on a date with her boyfriend, she accepted the ride. Several beers and sleeping pills later, the two were at an abandoned mine shaft near Weaver Lake. He raped her barely conscious body after beating her with the hammer as he had done before. After burning her purse, Olson returned to the car. He had gotten it stuck in some gravel and could not get it out. He approached a couple that he had seen on the way in, and they towed his truck for $20.

Ada was reported missing but, unlike the others, she seemed less likely to be a runaway in the eyes of police. Her family life was very stable and she did not have the elements that made the other missing kids so easy to dismiss. Despite the two bodies found and other kids reported missing, the police were still not considering amongst themselves that this could be a serial killer situation. All of these cases were still coincidental at this point.

On July 2, a 9-year-old boy named Simon Partington went missing. Olson noticed Simon riding his bike out of his driveway. He initially thought Simon was a young girl but was just as intrigued by the prospect of a young boy. He offered Simon a job, a ride, and a beer. He also gave him a sleeping pill. Since Simon was so young and small, he did not require the level of drugging that Olson's previous victims had.

Olson drove Simon just across from where he had previously murdered Christine. He didn't have a hammer with him. Instead, he used a buck knife and a belt to stab and asphyxiate the young boy. Simon's body was thrown in the river and Olson drove back to work. Within a few hours, Simon was reported missing and more than 100 people were out looking for him. People began to panic as the media outlets began flowing with speculation about the boy's disappearance. Simon's case was different than the others. He was still a young child. He could not just be dismissed as another angry teenager.

It was during this time that the officer in charge of Burnaby RCMP Detachment Sex Crimes Unit, Les Forsythe, became convinced, like Kettles, that Olson was their serial killer. Forsythe had been put in charge of Ada Court's disappearance and was certain that she hadn't run away.

Forsythe first noticed Olson's name because he had recently been charged for sexually assaulting a 16-year-old girl. That girl was named Sandra Docker. The day after Simon was murdered, Sandra and her friend, Rose Smythe, were at an arcade when Olson offered them both a job. They got in his car and Olson gave them beer while he drove around and pretended to show them their new job sites.

He arranged to pick up the girls a few days later on July 6. After driving around and drinking for a short while, he told Rose that she would have to go. He said that he only had enough work for one of them that day. Sandra was to be his unlucky "employee."

When she refused to have sex with Olson, he let her back out at the arcade where he had originally picked her up. She reported him to the police and he was arrested within a few minutes by the Surrey RCMP. Hearing of the assault in Surrey, Forsythe was sent out from Burnaby to speak with Olson.

Forsythe immediately felt uncomfortable in Olson's presence, and he quickly began to make connections amongst the various murders. Sandra had been picked up quite close to where both Ada and Daryn had gone missing. Forsythe even realized that Olson lived across the street from Ada's brother, where she had been right before she disappeared.

Forsythe began to investigate Olson's criminal record. He could not help but notice the significant number of charges against him relating to sexual offenses against young people of both genders. Because Olson had never actually been convicted of one of these offenses, he had gone largely unnoticed as a suspect for these other sex-related crimes. After an unsuccessful questioning of Olson, Forsythe put together a report that put Olson forth as a serious suspect for Daryn's and Ada's murders, and perhaps many other missing kids reports. Christine Weller was still forgotten at this point.

Around the same time, Olson had recently met Randy Ludlow and was letting the homeless teen stay at his house. On July 9, Olson and Randy approached a young woman at a pay phone. The girl was 14-year-old Judy Kozma. Judy had actually met Olson before. He had offered her a job but then he never showed up at the time they planned to meet. He forgot that she had written her name in his notebook as a reminder to meet her. Since she refused the car ride that first time they met, Olson moved on to other prey and forgot all about her. When Olson tried to chat her up, Judy instantly scolded him for having bailed on her. He apologized and asked that she get in the car so that they could talk about it.

The three of them began drinking and went to a McDonald's for some food. Olson told Randy to leave him and Judy alone and dropped Randy off at the mall. Judy took the sleeping pills and shortly fell asleep. Olson then drove to the same area where he had murdered Ada. Olson woke Judy up, but she immediately began to vomit. He beat her with his fists until she was unconscious and then raped her. Once he finished, Olson took Judy to the side of the riverbank. He took out his hunting knife and stabbed Judy a total of 19 times. He put some branches over her naked body and then drove a short distance to burn her clothes on a picnic table. He also took Judy's jewelry and added it to the spot where he had previously stashed Ada's jewelry. He then threw the knife away and hit the highway.

Olson stopped to make a phone call to Joan and told her they were going to take a vacation to California. When he did get home, Joan discovered Olson cleaning his hammer in the bathtub. She asked him why he was doing such a strange thing and his response was irritable enough that she backed off. They left for California the next day.

A Bad Vacation and Another Murder

While on the trip to California, Olson consistently bothered Joan about money. She had some money saved up to repay a loan she had been given by her father. Olson was very frustrated that she refused to give him the money. He coerced her by threatening to hurt their baby, Stephen.

Joan had returned from running errands one day only to find that Olson had cut their son with a knife just below his heart. The baby was covered in blood and Olson had left him like that in the crib to send Joan a message. He was not above doing unimaginably horrible things in order to get what he wanted. The scar remained on Stephen's body as he aged.

The same day, Olson also threatened to drown Stephen in the hotel pool. Olson took the baby from Joan and went deep into the pool. Making sure that Joan was watching, Olson held baby Stephen under the water. A lifeguard ran over as Joan began to scream and Olson pulled Stephen up. Later that day, she went to the bank and handed over the money to Olson. It wasn't worth the risk.

Before they reached their destination of Disneyland, Olson forced Joan to turn around and head back to B.C. Joan later suspected that Olson might have murdered an underage sex worker who she had spotted Olson talking to on the day he decided to leave. He left the hotel to run an errand for Joan but then stayed out for several hours. Joan also noticed that was the night that Olson's knife he always wore went missing.

On July 23, Olson was driving home from an unsuccessful attempt to lure a young woman from the unemployment office in New Westminster. As he passed a bus stop, Olson noticed 15-year-old Raymond King leaving the bus. He offered Raymond a job and the young teen got in the car. They eventually stopped at a phone so that Raymond could let his sister know that he had gotten a job. Olson eavesdropped and was pleased that Raymond hadn't said anything that could potentially incriminate him after he killed the boy.

Once Raymond was drunk and high, Olson drove back to Weaver Lake, where he had previously killed Judy and Ada. After raping Raymond, Olson hammered a 3-inch nail into his head as he lay on his stomach. Raymond didn't die immediately, but Olson raped him anyway. Afterward, Olson threw Raymond's body into a ravine and tossed boulders at it to ensure that he was completely dead. He then threw logs and branches down until he felt like the body was sufficiently hidden. Five hours later, Raymond's father reported him missing to the RCMP.

The Serious Suspect and The German Girl

Olson did not know that at this point he had already become a more serious suspect. After both Maile and Forsythe had independently pushed for him as the suspect in two separate murders, the RCMP began to consider the case they made for him. Right before Olson and Joan left for California, Maile had approached a friend of Joan's to ask about Olson. He said to let him know when they returned. Maile was hoping to organize surveillance for Olson. However, members of the RCMP were reluctant to do so because surveillance was very costly and surveillance officers cannot make arrests if they see someone committing a crime.

The night of Raymond's murder, Detective Dennis Tarr came to Olson's apartment and asked to speak with him. Olson had previously contacted Tarr hoping to get on payroll as an informer about some robberies (likely ones he actually committed himself). Tarr and Olson spoke extensively, and eventually the topic turned to Simon Partington. Olson was very curious and pried Tarr for information. What he didn't realize was that Tarr was actually scoping out Olson as a suspect and was not actually interested in hiring him as an informer.

Detective Fred Maile had been working with a man named Ed Drozda who worked in the Serious Crimes unit of the RCMP. Tarr had previously mentioned Olson to them both when Olson first asked about becoming an informant. They requested Tarr check out Olson for them under the pretense of perhaps hiring him. However, Olson had such a relaxed demeanor that Tarr was unsure what to make of him. Tarr advised Maile and Drozda that they should set up a meeting with Olson themselves.

On July 25, Judy Kozma's body was discovered by a group of hikers. Only two days earlier, the RCMP had authorized surveillance to begin on Olson, but it had not gone into effect yet. They were getting worried. Despite searching the scene extensively and circulating photos of Olson, the RCMP were not having any luck directly linking Olson to the crime.

On July 24, Olson murdered yet another youth. This time, it was an 18-year-old exchange student from Germany named Sigrun Arnd. Olson spotted Sigrun on the side of the road and offered her a ride to Burnaby. He took Sigrun to meet some guys he knew at a pub. They all had some beers and Sigrun was delighted at the opportunity to practice her English in authentic conversation.

When Olson and Sigrun returned to the car, he offered her another beer and slipped the sleeping pills into it. He drove her to the same area where he had previously killed Christine and Simon. They began to walk towards a more secluded space by the train tracks, and Olson used his hammer to knock Sigrun off her feet. He began to rape her. Suddenly, Olson heard a train whistle and noticed a man who was jogging just behind the train. Olson waved to the brakeman and he waved back. When speaking with police later, the brakeman explained that he had thought it was just a couple having sex. Since Sigrun was so knocked out at this point, she missed the opportunity to get help. Olson beat her again with the hammer and then buried her dead body in a ditch filled with mud.

Murdering Under Surveillance

On July 27, 1981, Olson picked up 15-year-old Terri Lyn Carson. With the usual routine, Olson trapped Terri and drove her with him to Hope. In Hope, he cashed some traveler's checks that he had stolen from Sigrun. He then killed Terri by hammering a screwdriver into her head just off the highway near Agassiz.

That same day, the RCMP surveillance of Olson was finally underway. Unfortunately, they were not following him when he murdered Terri. Instead, they had parked outside of his apartment building and were waiting for him to return. They spent the next day following Olson around, but he was uncharacteristically behaving himself. To save money, the RCMP had only budgeted for surveillance to occur during the day. There were concerns that Olson was aware he was being watched and therefore kept his activities clean during the daytime. In reality, Olson felt invincible and was oblivious to the fact that he was under surveillance.

Unable to catch him misbehaving, the surveillance was called off on July 28. On July 29, Tarr notified Maile and Drozda that he had set up a meeting with Olson and Randy at a spot called the Caribou Inn. Maile, Drozda, and other surveillance posted up nearby to watch how the meeting went. When Olson and Randy arrived, they were not dressed appropriately for the standards of the Caribou Inn. The meeting was then moved to White Spot.

Tarr spoke to Olson and said that what he was really after was information on missing kids. Olson had long been plotting to murder and frame Randy for his other murders, and this seemed like a perfect opportunity to do so. He demanded $3,000 per month to provide the police with the desired information. Tarr agreed but only if Olson would speak with other RCMP members.

Forty minutes after the meeting ended, Olson and Randy were arrested trying to pick up some hitchhiking kids. However, without a proper arrest warrant, Olson had to be released. Surveillance was reinstated, and over the next few days, undercover cops saved several children.

The surveillance police could not arrest Olson, but they were able to pretend to be the guardians of whatever child he would target. Nonetheless, surveillance was once again called off due to budget concerns. Furthermore, the RCMP were also nervous because the negotiations to make him an informant were now underway. They did not want the surveillance to scare Olson from helping them.

The Beast Is Finally Caught

Olson met with Tarr, Maile, and Drozda on the morning of July 30. Olson assessed Maile as being the kind of man he could easily manipulate. Maile purposely spoke very slowly so as to give Olson the impression that he wasn't as smart as Olson himself. Maile knew that if he got Olson to trust him, Olson would probably let something slip in the midst of trying to be charming. Maile convinced Olson that if he could give them the whereabouts of bodies and a killer, they would pay him a significant sum of money. He also promised to give Olson a new identity and to relocate his family as part of witness protection.

When the meeting ended, Olson's surveillance was still not reinstated. He left his meeting with the police and picked up his last victim, a 17-year-old named Louise Marie Chartrand. After raping the drugged girl in a secluded area, something surprising happened. Louise openly accused Olson of intending to murder her.

He was taken aback. None of the other kids had ever called him out before. They had all been too intoxicated to realize or accept the nature of their fate. Olson got angry and defended himself. He said that he hadn't raped her and that their sex was consensual. This was always his reaction when someone would accuse him of being a rapist. Olson hated being called a rapist and a pedophile and would always react defensively whenever someone called him that. Now that Louise was accusing him, he felt the same way.

Olson indignantly denied planning to kill her. However, Louise spotted his knife and tried to stab him with it before he could grab it. Olson grabbed her arm and threatened to break her wrist if she didn't let go. Louise asked Olson to promise he wouldn't kill her if she dropped the knife. He promised. Louise left the car to pee and as she squatted, Olson hit her in the back of the head with the hammer. He buried her body under some gravel and drove away as fast as he could. He even passed a police car as he left the scene of the crime. He left with Joan for Alberta the next day.

On August 5, Raymond King's body was found. Two days later, RCMP had finally tracked down Olson since the day he had murdered Louise. At long last, he was under surveillance 24 hours a day.

On August 12, the RCMP arrested Olson. He was on Vancouver Island and had picked up two young girls who were hitchhiking. Not wanting to wait until something more sinister happened, the RCMP moved in while the three were having a picnic in a forest. Luckily for the police, they seized Olson's notebook and found the evidence they needed to justify his arrest. Judy Kozma's name was written within the pages of his notebook. It was the first and only major evidential link they had between Olson and a victim.

Police later got testimony from Randy that he had been with Olson when Judy was picked up. Around the time that he had murdered Louise, Olson brutally raped Randy after drugging him. Olson had brought Randy to an alleyway behind a strip mall off of the highway. After failing to break into the mall, Olson decided instead to take Randy back to the house and assault him there. Randy was traumatized from the experience and wanted nothing to do with Olson after that event. In retrospect, Randy felt that Olson had been trying to murder him that night.

Life Imprisonment and Finally Death

Olson was questioned by police but remained evasive. He insisted that he knew all the people whose names were written in his notebook. The police then questioned him about Judy Kozma's name being in his notebook. Olson realized he had been tricked. He responded by asking for his lawyer, Bob Shantz.

Shantz advised Olson not to take bail. Shantz believed that Olson was likely not guilty of the murders since his previous record was mostly related to burglaries and breaking and entering. He told Olson that he should cooperate with the police and answer all questions until they realized that he was innocent.

Days went on with Olson being interrogated constantly. The police used all manner of different tactics and personalities, but Olson would not break. He would only maintain that he knew some things about the murders. He did not implicate himself directly, which was what the police needed. One day while speaking with Maile, Olson began to speak about himself in third person. He began to insinuate that if he could get an insanity plea, he would cooperate.

Maile called in Inspector Proke who was the head of the Serious Crimes unit. Proke spoke with Olson and set up a trap for him. He told Olson that before they agreed to an insanity charge that they would need to know the location of at least one hidden body. Olson was not to be fooled so easily. He knew that they would charge him as soon as he gave them a body.

Proke and Olson talked in circles for a while. Neither of them wanted to give too much away. Proke finally came out and asked Olson why he did it. Without thinking, Olson responded, "It was the pills and the drinking. I might have been drunk, but I always knew what I was doing. I mean, my friend always knew. It's him I'm talking about." Proke and Olson agreed to a deal. Proke convinced Olson that if he gave them the bodies, he would ensure that Olson was put in a psychiatric hospital as opposed to a prison.

Shantz was furious that Olson would make a deal. He told Olson that the police were lying to him. The police had no ability to promise him an insanity plea. By agreeing to help find the bodies, Olson was agreeing to his own guilt as the murderer. Shantz told Olson that they would go to trial and that doing so would get him free.

Instead of heeding his lawyer's advice, Olson and the RCMP made what would become a media scandal known as the "cash for bodies" deal. The deal was that Joan would receive $100,000 in exchange for Olson divulging the whereabouts of 11 bodies. It was realistically the only method the police had to get the evidence needed to prosecute Olson. However, this was largely because of their failure to accurately gather evidence on him prior to the arrest. Olson managed to commit four murders in the week after Forsythe had already recommended him for constant surveillance. One of those murders he committed a few hours after having a meeting with the RCMP. This all reflected terribly on the police.

In fairness to the RCMP, the deal was initially planned to be fake. The man in charge of the Olson investigation, Bruce Northorp, sent a message to Ottawa containing a note that they were signing the deal without it being legally binding and with the intention to recover the money after all the bodies were found. Northorp discussed with his federal superiors several options for recovering the money. These included through use of a search warrant, to charge Olson with extortion, to recover the money through criminal activity, or to say that the RCMP entered the deal while under duress.

Olson was examined by a psychiatric doctor and, despite his best efforts, was found fit to stand trial set for January 11, 1982. On August 26, Olson took police to begin digging out the bodies of the other victims. He was set up at Oakalla prison where he had spent so much time before. Guards and prisoners alike abused him by throwing cups of pee at him, punching him, and spitting on him. Olson later complained about his clothes getting ruined by all the pee that was thrown at him. He successfully sued and got financially rewarded for it.

The Trial

On January 11, 1982, Olson finally went to trial. There were fifty different media outlets present. Only the families of Judy Kozma and Terri Lyn Carson attended. Olson pleaded not guilty to the ten murder charges against him. On January 13, Tarr submitted evidence of their recorded conversations in White Spot. Olson decided to change his plea. The next day, he formally pleaded guilty. What was expected to be a long-winded trial was over in only a few days. He was sentenced to life imprisonment with parole consideration after 25 years.

People were still outraged. On one hand, many believed the sentence was too short. One MP from Alberta even introduced a bill so that an exception to the canceled death penalty could be made solely for Olson. The bill was not successful.

After the trial, the "cash for bodies" deal became public. At first, the Attorney General denied that he knew about its existence. He then retired once the media began attacking him for blatantly lying.

Daryn's stepfather, Gary Rosenfeldt, was particularly upset about the "cash for bodies" deal. Speaking out in 1986, Rosenfeldt said, "This decision gives an open invitation to murderers and other criminals to set up a trust fund to benefit from their crimes...the people of Canada won't stand for this."

Rosenfeldt created an organization called Victims of Violence that grew to become an important organization for providing support to the families of kids who are murdered. Rosenfeldt mobilized other families of Olson's victims to take Joan to court for the money she received. It seemed despicable that the family of this monster could financially profit off of their suffering. Yet, the court ruled in Joan's favor. Even though Joan did not deserve it, the police could not rescind on their deal. She and Stephen got to keep the money. If Joan had a stronger conscience, she would have given that money over to the other families. However, after many years of her own suffering, she probably felt Olson owed her something too.

The families of Olson's victims received no financial recompense. The only exception to this was Terri Lyn's mother, Terry Carson. Her welfare payments were cut in half and she was forced to move from her house because she was no longer living as a family. After her ordeal became public, the Human Resources Minister of B.C. gave Terry $4,000 from the Criminal Injuries Compensation Board.

Olson was sent to the federal penitentiary in Kingston, Ontario. He immediately proposed doing another deal for more bodies. He also approached various people to help write a memoir. Olson said that he would give the profits from its sale to families of his victims. This was something they obviously did not want. In the United States, the "Son of Sam" law prevents a criminal from profiting off of the publication of their crimes. At the time, it was considered a violation of the Canadian Charter of Rights to create such a similar law in Canada. However, to prevent such actions by Olson, the Solicitor-General Robert Kaplan prohibited Olson from having any contact with the media. It was useless. Olson still managed to violate this rule many times.

Other Victims?

In terms of the "new bodies" deal, there were many suspicions that Olson had several other victims. In later interviews, he admitted to killing kids while traveling through the United States with Joan. However, he never gave tangible evidence that he had. There were also several other women in Canada who seemed like they could be legitimate victims.

The most notable of these was Debbie Silverman. Debbie Silverman was a 21-year-old woman who lived in Toronto. On the night of August 11, 1978, Debbie went out to a bar with some friends from work. She brought a date along with her to the party. It was a young man from her work.

In the early hours of the morning around 5 a.m., Debbie returned home in her car. Residents in the building reported having heard a loud scream. Her purse and jewelry were dropped in the corridor of the ground floor of the apartment building.

Another resident found it the next morning and returned the purse along with her car key and credit cards. He stole her jewelry and cash and then left the other items outside of her door.

Debbie's sister, Karen, lived in the same apartment. Karen went to leave the apartment the next morning and discovered the purse. Knowing that Debbie did not return the previous night, Karen immediately called the police. Three months later, Debbie's body was found just off a highway to the north of Toronto.

In 1984 while imprisoned, Olson signed a "Statement of Facts" claiming that he was responsible for Debbie's murder. The statement described in lurid detail how Olson claimed he murdered Debbie. Olson sent this statement to several people over the years. No one responded because they assumed he was merely doing it for attention. It also didn't help that at some points Olson would change his story such that he only witnessed the murder.

There were also issues with his story because Olson was supposed to be in the United States when Debbie was murdered. Olson then stated he returned to Toronto just for the one day that he murdered Debbie, a doubtful claim. However, Olson did seem to know too much for comfort about how she was murdered. He included details in his statement that were never presented to the media. These details included the exact jewelry she wore, that her hands were tied behind her back, that she was only partially naked, and that a halter had been left around her neck.

Olson offered to take a lie detector test several times regarding the matter. However, every time a crew was sent over to test him, he refused to do it. Olson also forwarded the RCMP a letter that was supposedly addressed to him from someone named Ronnie. In the letter, Ronnie warned Olson not to tell anyone about Debbie Silverman. There was no return address on the letter and it was sent from Surrey. Since Olson would not divulge any more details about who Ronnie was, the police were very skeptical. It could easily have been a ruse in which Olson persuaded someone to write and mail this letter on his behalf.

After Olson confessed, another known serial killer from the United States also confessed to Debbie's murder. However, this man did not seem to know any of the details of how she was killed. All of the information he provided was completely inaccurate. It was later discovered that there was no way this other man could have killed Debbie. Her murder was never solved.

In 1982, Olson wrote to the Solicitor-General that he knew murder details and the whereabouts of bodies for several other women and two males. In response to this, Maile was sent to interrogate Olson. With Shantz present, Olson claimed to know about the deaths of Helen Hopcraft, Gail Ann Weys, Marnie Jamieson, Pamela Darlington, Verna Bjerky, Carmen Robinson, and Robert Dallum. Some of these he was able to give interesting details about. Others, he was too vague or inconsistent in his story.

Throughout the interrogation, Olson kept referencing his knowledge of murders that occurred in the United States. However, the RCMP had no interest in his American murders. It was not within their jurisdiction to investigate or negotiate on behalf of American authorities. Olson variously claimed to have murdered people in Chicago, Seattle, Miami, Hawaii, and elsewhere. In total, he claimed to have either killed or known the details of 27 murders in the United States. The validity of these claims remains unknown to this day.

The outcome of the interrogation with Maile was that Olson got a deal of sorts. Olson had been hoping that any deal would be a replication of his previous one. He would get $10,000 for every body he gave. However, the backlash from the previous deal was so great that there was no chance it could ever happen again. Olson then asked to be transferred from Kingston penitentiary to a facility in British Columbia. The deal they eventually worked out was that Olson would be returned to B.C. only if he gave details about the various murders and locations of evidence. In return, he would get to have a visit with Joan and Stephen.

Unfortunately for the RCMP, the media found out about the new deal. The chaos that followed led the RCMP to call the body search off. It was too complicated. While in B.C., the Attorney General ordered that Olson's jail cell be raided for information. By the time the raid occurred, Olson had already given all of his documents over to his lawyer. Furthermore, the raid violated the Canadian Charter of Rights as well as the parameters of the negotiations with Olson. The raid was both illegal and fruitless. After this incident, the RCMP never again tried to negotiate with Olson for information.

Fun In Prison

During imprisonment, Olson continued to harass people with his inappropriate actions. With the rush of killing and rape taken from him, he had to fill his compulsive need for drama some other way. He was constantly in pursuit of attention and would take any manner of routes to get it.

One of his favorite games was to cut out photos of women from porn magazines and mail them to various political and legal authorities. He would claim that these women were his girlfriends and would request conjugal visits with them. Obviously, Olson was not supposed to have access to pornography in prison, let alone the ability to mail it. It was just another of the countless examples in which it came to light that Olson's supervision was inadequate.

Similarly, in 1992, Olson forged a letter from the future prime minister, Kim Campbell. The letter said that she was sending him naked photos and that she wished to have sex with him. Other recipients of mail from Clifford Olson included more than 100 female pen pals, journalists, the Pope, and the families of his victims. These pen pals would often send Olson money, which he then used to buy a cable television, a computer, a cellphone, a video recorder, and a tape recorder.

In May 1986, Olson sent a letter to the family of Daryn Johnsrude in which he detailed the manner of how he killed their teenaged son. He likely targeted Daryn's family because of the high profile that was kept by Gary Rosenfeldt through his work as a victim's rights advocate. At one point, Olson also filed a lawsuit against Daryn's mother, Sharon Rosenfeldt. He cited defamation of character as the grounds for his suit.

In 2011, Sharon told the media, "We feel strongly that had justice worked in the manner it was supposed to work, 30 years ago, Clifford Olson would have been in jail serving time for other sex crimes that went unattended, that were stayed by the courts, and I feel that the justice system helped create the monster that he became and my son paid for this with his life."

One of the journalists with whom Olson maintained a relationship was named Arlene Bynon. He noticed Bynon during a television appearance in which she discussed serial killer Ted Bundy. After that, Olson and Bynon began a long-term correspondence. They would write letters, have phone conversations, and Olson would mail her videos of himself.

In one such video, Olson pretended to be a reporter covering an issue inside of the penitentiary. Bynon later remarked that she actually found him to be a good reporter. Perhaps all the media attention had given him a flair for it. After reading *Silence of the Lambs*, Olson wrote to Bynon with implications that he regarded her as the Clarice Starling to his Hannibal Lecter. Upon reflection years later, Bynon admits that while she experienced the enormous evil residing in Olson, she still appreciated some of his more charming antics.

In 1990, Olson was also caught in possession of illegal drugs in his cell. When sentenced to life in prison, getting caught with drugs seems inconsequential.

Nonetheless, Olson was charged with possession for having 8 grams of hash. It was an ironic turn of events since his days of ratting out other inmates with drugs.

Joan finally divorced Olson by 1991 and remarried. She and Stephen moved elsewhere in British Columbia. They kept away from the public eye and hopefully managed some semblance of a normal life.

During 1982, Olson filled several notebooks writing down all the intricate details of his murders. It was just like when he convinced Marcoux to do the same activity. It had to be perfect. Olson dedicated the writings to Stephen. He explained his reasoning: "I don't want Stephen to learn about his dad from others, I want him to understand what his dad was thinking, then he might understand better and, by understanding, come to love and forgive..." Considering his desire to write a memoir on the subject, it is more likely that Olson was hoping to use them for that purpose. Because he was prohibited from contacting people to write on his behalf, he probably decided he could say he was giving them to his son. It is unknown whether Stephen ever accepted this twisted gift from his father.

In 1992, Olson partially attempted one of his many infamous escapes from prison. It was quite similar to the escape attempt he made in 1965. While getting an X-ray at the Hotel Dieu Hospital in Kingston, Olson was found to be hiding the key to both his handcuffs and leg irons. He had swallowed the key, ostensibly in hopes of excreting it out while alone in a washroom. However, he did not have the chance to do so before getting the X-ray. Olson may not have even believed he could get away with such an elaborate plan. Even if he did manage to unlock himself in a bathroom, someone would be waiting for him on the other side of the door. For Olson, it was enough of a delight for him to cheekily highlight the incompetency of his authorities.

In 1997, it came to light that Olson had made videotapes with the same content as his writings for Stephen. In 1993, Olson and his warden Jim O'Sullivan signed a contract that allowed Olson to make 12 videos of himself describing his murders. The tapes were supposed to be for legal purposes and were to be given to the RCMP, the FBI, and Correctional Services Canada. The contract also allowed for Olson to send the videotapes to Shantz.

This posed an issue because if Shantz was in possession of the tapes, there was a chance that Olson could direct his lawyer to give them to the media. Shantz spoke publicly that he would never release the tapes, even if Olson requested him to do so. The CSC and the Solicitor-General at the time were also adamant that Olson did not have copyright for the tape. However, nothing in the contract actually supported that claim. Olson registered the tapes for copyright in 1995, with hopes that they would be made into a television series. He entitled them "Motivational, Sexual Homicide Patterns of Serial Killer Clifford Robert Olson." Only some of the tapes were delivered to Shantz, and so Olson filed a suit against the CSC in order to get the remainder sent to his lawyer. Olson lost his legal battle for the tapes after a judge ruled that Olson should not have had access to a camera in the first place.

Also in 1997, Olson created yet another stir by applying for early parole through what was called the faint hope clause. The faint hope clause was Section 745 of the Criminal Code. It allowed for murderers in prison to apply for parole after 15 years if they were successfully pursuing their rehabilitation. Almost no one had ever tried to make use of the clause, much less any serial killers like Olson. Olson knew that there was no way he would ever be granted parole. He went through the hassle of applying simply to waste people's time and to garner media attention.

Olson's witnesses whom he called to speak on his behalf were two psychiatrists. One of them was Dr. Anthony Marcus. "He is undoubtedly an incorrigible anti social personality...totally recalcitrant to change," he said of Olson. Both psychiatrists went on to say that Olson should never be released from prison, as he was likely to murder again. After their testimonies, Olson said he was pleased with both of their assessments.

He then went on to claim that he could directly incriminate members of the RCMP along with more than one Prime Minister for ruining and foiling murder investigations. Of course, Olson did not get the parole he sought. However, media reports of the incident displayed the photographs of him smiling on his way to the hearing. Geoff Pevere from The Toronto Star aptly wrote, "...We made his day. And his smile must be taken as a chilling gesture of gratitude." The faint hope clause was repealed in 2011 when the Serious Time for The Most Serious Crime Act was passed. Olson was the last serial killer in Canada to legally ask for early parole through the clause.

Olson's parole hearing in 2006 did not go much better. He angrily scolded the parole board for having released other serial killers back into society. "In my opinion, serial killers should never be paroled. That is my opinion. I'm not trying to be facetious or smart or being a jackass, or anything," he said.

As the hearing progressed, Olson claimed that the U.S. Department of Homeland Security had already granted him immunity and that therefore the Canadian government had no jurisdiction over him. This supposed "immunity" was apparently related to 9/11. Olson had declared that in June of 1999 he mailed a letter to the American government with the following information:

"I have been contacted by the following students who are from ... Kabul in Afghanistan. They have all been living here in Montreal, Canada, and then went to the United States as students in the University of Florida ... In their letters they state that all belong to the fundamentalist Muslim and some group called AL-Qaida in Afghanistan and that some of them will be coming to Canada and then the United States to take some pilot training on jets ... They talk in these letters about these guys going to do some kind of terrorism with a air plane in New York state."

Before the break at the hearing, Olson said he wasn't actually interested in getting parole. "I will be staying in my cell, I won't be coming back to hear your retarded decision," he said. When the hearing ended, that "retarded decision" was of course to keep Olson in prison.

These parole hearings were more than just a waste of people's time and an opportunity for Olson to get attention. Many of his victims' families had complained to media that Olson could get hearings as frequently as every two years. Every time he had a hearing, they had to relive their experiences either through victim impact statements or simply through notification that he was granted a hearing at all. In March of 2011, legal changes were made so that there were much longer wait times between parole hearings for multiple murderers.

In 2010, it came to light that Olson was one of many prisoners collecting Old Age Security along with Guaranteed Income Supplement payments from the government. Luckily, Olson was only receiving Old Age Security for a short period of time before it became public knowledge. Media and citizens were outraged that Olson was receiving $1,200 each month from the government. The money went into a trust fund for Olson, although it is unclear how and if he was using the money. Speaking publicly on the matter, then Prime Minister Stephen Harper said, "I've read all the recent stories in the papers about Mr. Olson, and I must admit that I'm as upset by this, as concerned about this, as any other Canadian." In his typically cheeky manner, Olson mailed his check to Harper, hoping to make a donation to the Conservative party. Enclosed with the check was a request: "May I please receive a tax receipt from the Conservative Party of Canada."

The Prime Minister's director of communications commented, "We will not accept one penny from a reprehensible child killer." Unsurprisingly, Harper's office returned the check to Olson. On Olson's birthday in 2011, the Canadian government made a legal amendment that senior prisoners could no longer collect security benefits while imprisoned.

Finally, in 2011, Olson's cancer diagnosis became public. He spent a month receiving treatment at the Archambault hospital center in Saint Annes de Plaines, Quebec. The hospital was attached to the federal prison complex where Olson lived. He died on September 30, 2011, and was buried in a secret ceremony and location. It was an anticlimactic end to a life spent hurting other people. At the time of his death, he had spent almost 50 of his 71 years imprisoned. Families of victims were finally able to feel some small relief from the burden of his existence. His constant cries for attention over the years had prohibited them from properly moving on from their tragedies. Ada Court's sister, Trudy, said, "These are tears of happiness, because justice is done for the children. Our justice system couldn't do it for them. But life has. He's gone now."

Not all of his victims' families could declare the same feelings. After struggling with depression from losing his daughter, Colleen Daignault's father committed suicide in 1986. Her stepmother, Dee Johnston, spoke to the media a few days before Olson died. "For anyone who thinks this is closure, it is not." Johnston's words reflected the reality that there is no real way to feel closure from such horrible losses. Even with Olson dead, his legacy as one of Canada's most despicable killers will remain forever.

About The Author

Elizabeth Broderick grew up in British Columbia but currently lives in Toronto where she attends university. She became interested in true crime after reading about Charles Manson and his followers. When she isn't writing or studying, she can be found supporting craft breweries, making pickles, and working on a sustainability project for her school.

"If you enjoyed reading this book, please take a moment to leave a brief review on Amazon, Goodreads and any other market. Your feedback is very important to the author and publisher."

Thank you,

Elizabeth

RJ Parker / Peter Vronsky (VP Publications)

About Crimes Canada: True Crimes That Shocked the Nation

This is a multi-volume twenty-four book, (one per month, each approximately 100 to 180 pages) project by crime historian Dr. Peter Vronsky and true crime author and publisher RJ Parker, depicting some of Canada's most notorious criminals.

Crimes Canada: True Crimes that Shocked the Nation will feature a series of Canadian true crime short-read books published by *VP Publications* (Vronsky & Parker), an imprint of *RJ Parker Publishing, Inc.*, one of North America's leading publishers of true crime.

Peter Vronsky is the bestselling author of *Serial Killers: The Method and Madness of Monsters* and *Female Serial Killers: How and Why Women Become Monsters* while RJ Parker is not only a successful publisher but also the author of 18 books, including *Serial Killers Abridged: An Encyclopedia of 100 Serial Killers*, *Parents Who Killed Their*

Children: Filicide, and _Serial Killer Groupies_. Both are Canadians and have teamed up to share shocking Canadian true crime cases not only with fellow Canadian readers but with Americans and world readers as well, who will be shocked and horrified by just how evil and sick "nice" Canadians can be when they go bad.

Finally, we invite fellow Canadians, aspiring or established authors, to submit proposals or manuscripts to _VP Publications_ at _Editors@CrimesCanada.com_.

VP Publications is a new frontier traditional publisher, offering their published authors a generous royalty agreement payable within three months of publishing and aggressive online marketing support. Unlike many so-called "publishers" that are nothing but vanity presses in disguise, VP Publications does not charge authors in advance for submitting their proposal or manuscripts, nor do we charge authors if we choose to publish their works. We pay you, and pay well.

Acknowledgments

Thank you to my editor, proof-readers, and cover artist for your support:

- - Elizabeth Broderick

Aeternum Designs (book cover), Bettye McKee (editor), Dr. Peter Vronsky (editor), RJ Parker Publishing, VP Publications, Lorrie Suzanne Phillippe, Marlene Fabregas, Darlene Horn, Ron Steed, Katherine McCarthy, Robyn MacEachern, Kim Jackson, Lee Knieper Husemann, Kathi Garcia, Vicky Matson-Carruth, Cynthia Wood, Amanda Hutchins, and Linda H. Bergeron

Books in the Crimes Canada Collection

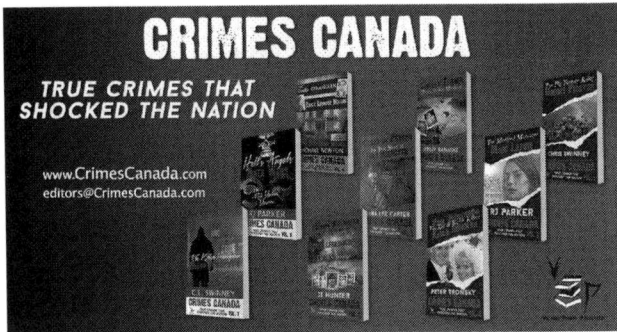

An exciting 24-volume series collection, edited by crime historian Dr. Peter Vronsky and true crime author and publisher RJ Parker.

VOLUMES:

(URL LINK ON NEXT PAGE)

1. Robert Pickton: The Pig Farmer Killer by C.L. Swinney

2. Marc Lepine: The Montreal Massacre by RJ Parker

3. Paul Bernardo and Karla Homolka by Peter Vronsky

4. Shirley Turner: Doctor, Stalker, Murderer by Kelly Banaski

5. Canadian Psycho: Luka Magnotta by Cara Lee Carter

6. The Country Boy Killer: Cody Legebokoff by JT Hunter

7. The Killer Handyman by C.L. Swinney

8. Hell's Angels Biker Wars by RJ Parker

9. The Dark Strangler by Michael Newton

10. The Alcohol Murders by Harriet Fox

11. Peter Woodcock: Canada's Youngest Serial Killer by Mark Bourrie

View these and future books in this collection at:

rjpp.ca/CC-CRIMES-CANADA-BOOKS

References

Bartholomew, Kim, Katherine Regan, Doug Oram, and Monica A. White. "Correlates of Partner Abuse in Male Same-Sex Relationships." *Violence and Victims* 23.3 (2008): 344-60. *ProQuest*. Web. 1 Sept. 2015.

Bynon, Arlene. "My Time With The Monster." *Toronto Star*. July 2006: A4. Web. 1 Sept. 2015.

"Serial Killer Clifford Olson Dies." *CBC News*. The Canadian Press, 30 Sept. 2011. Web. 1 Sept. 2015.

"Clifford Olson, Coming to a Video Store Near You? His Jailers Deny They Granted Him Copyright of Dubious Confessional Recording." *British Columbia Report* 8.18 (1996): 22-23. *ProQuest*. Web. 1 Sept. 2015.

"Day May Move to Control Prisoner 'Murderabilia'" *CTV News*. The Canadian Press, 29 July 2008. Web. 1 Sept. 2015.

"Gary Rosenfeldt, Advocate for Crime Victims, Has Died." *CTV News*. The Canadian Press, 10 Feb. 2009. Web. 1 Sept. 2015.

Cunningham, Dave. "The Banality of Evil." *Alberta Report* 24.38 (1997): 28. *ProQuest*. Web. 1 Sept. 2015.

Diagnostic and Statistical Manual of Mental Disorders: DSM-5. Washington, D.C.: American Psychiatric Association, 2013. Print.

Farrow, Moira. "Telling New Facts About Olson Horror Case." *The Vancouver Sun* 18 Aug. 1990: D22. Web. 1 Sept. 2015.

Fong, Petti, and Josh Tapper. "Serial Killer Clifford Olson Dying of Cancer." *The Toronto Star*. 21 Sept. 2011. Web. 1 Sept. 2015.

Hager, Mike, and Thandi Fletcher. "Serial Child-Killer Clifford Olson Dying of Cancer: Victims' Families." *The Vancouver Sun*. Postmedia News, 21 Sept. 2011. Web. 1 Sept. 2015.

Holmes, W. Leslie, and Bruce Northorp. *Where Shadows Linger: The Untold Story of the RCMP's Olson Murder Investigation*. Surrey: Heritage House, 2000. Print.

Howard, Ross. "Olson's Faint Hope Grows Fainter: Two Psychiatric Witnesses Called By The Serial Killer Say He Should Never Be Released." 19 Aug. 1997: A4. *The Globe and Mail*. Web. 1 Sept. 2015.

Kaufmann, Bill. "Clifford Olson's Lethal Legacy." *Toronto Sun*. 21 Sept. 2011. Web. 1 Sept. 2015.

"He Has No Concept Of Reality." *Maclean's* 1 Sept. 1997: 31. *ProQuest*. Web. 1 Sept. 2015.

Lussier, Gordon. "Ex-Con Recalls Attempt to Kill Clifford Olson." Interview by Michelle Mandel. *Airdrieecho.com*. Sun News Network, 24 Sept. 2011. Web. 1 Sept. 2015.

Martin, Sandra. "The Life and Death of Clifford Olson." *The Globe and Mail*. 30 Sept. 2011. Web. 1 Sept. 2015.

Murray, John B. "Psychological Profile of Pedophiles and Child Molesters." *The Journal of Psychology* 134.2 (2000): 211-24. *Scholar's Portal.* Web. 1 Sept. 2015.

Pevere, Geoff. "How We Made His Day." *The Toronto Star* 29 Aug. 1997: A31. Print.

"Selling Memoirs in the U.S.: Olson." *The Globe and Mail* 20 May 1982: 11. Web. 1 Sept. 2015.

"I Didn't Know Beforehand of Cash-For-Bodies Deal: Olson's Wife." *The Montreal Gazette* 24 Oct. 1984: B7. *Google News.* Web. 1 Sept. 2015.

"Timeline for Killer Clifford Olson." *Toronto Sun.* QMI Agency, 21 Sept. 2011. Web. 1 Sept. 2015.

"Clifford Olson Wins Again: Allan Rock Continues To Makes Prisoners' Rights A Top Priority." *Western Report* 1 Apr. 1996: 20-21. *ProQuest.* Web. 1 Sept. 2015.

Worthington, Peter. *Predator: The Life and Crimes of Serial Killer Clifford Olson.* Peter Worthington, 2012. Kobo Edition.

Made in the USA
San Bernardino, CA
28 January 2017